Endorsements
OF CLAY CLARK

"Clay, you've become an influencer. More than anything else, you have evolved into an influencer where your word has more and more power. As you know, there is alot of fake influencers out there. I'm glad that you and I agree so much. You are on it man! Everybody listen to this guy. He knows what he's talking about."

- Robert Kiyosaki
(The best-selling author of The Rich Dad Poor Dad book series and a man who has sold over 40 million copies of his entrepreneur books.)

"Clay Clark is an entrepreneur extraordinaire."

- David Robinson
(NBA Hall of Basketball Player, former NBA MVP, NBA Championship Winner & Investor.)

"He's like Steve Martin meets Steve Forbes."

- Jim Stovall
(New York Times best-selling self-help writer best known for his bestselling novel The Ultimate Gift. The book was made into the movie The Ultimate Gift, distributed by 20th Century Fox. The Ultimate Gift has a prequel called The Ultimate Life and a sequel called The Ultimate Legacy.)

"For the last two years, I have come to Clay Clark's *Thrivetime Show* conference/seminar, and I must say I didn't know what to expect at first, but it's EXCEPTIONAL. If you are serious, and I mean really serious about your career, your entrepreneurship, and your wealth creation ability. I strongly, implore you to come to Tulsa, invest the two days, it will change your life. It's quite extraordinary, and I'm a tough grader."

- Michael Levine
(The publicist and public relations expert of choice for 58 Academy Award winners, 34 Grammy Award winners, and 43 New York Times best-sellers including Michael Jackson, Barbra Streisand, Prince, Nike, and others.)

PAWS, for a Notable Quotable

"The difference between great people and everyone else is that great people create their lives actively, while everyone else is created by their lives, passively waiting to see where life takes them next. The difference between the two is living fully and just existing."

-MICHAEL GERBER
(Best-selling author of The E-Myth Revisited)

FEATURING CELEBRITY DOG, "ACHILLES"

Make Your Dog Epic

Principles To Enhance Any Training Method

J.T. LAWSON & CLAY CLARK

(Author of *What I Learned from my Millionaire Mentor*. Real estate investor, lead trainer and owner of Make Your Dog Epic Oklahoma location.)

(Former U.S. SBA Young Entrepreneur of the Year, the 6x iTunes chart-topping podcast host of the ThrivetimeShow, and *Forbes* Coaches Council member, Clay Clark.)

> We provide website, answer initial calls, and branding, as well as offer other support you can access at will.

Happy Paw·lidays

Behold, An Epic, Mind-Expanding, Dog Training Festival Of Literary Wonder!

Make Your Dog Epic
Principles To Enhance Any Training Method

ISBN: 979-8-9908526-2-4

Copyright © by Clay Clark

Clay Clark Publishing
Published by Clay Clark Publishing
3920 West 91st Street South
Tulsa, OK 74132

There is a high probability that this book is printed in the United States of America. All rights not reserved. If you want to copy this book and share it with your friends and family that is fine with us.
Quick Note: You can teach an old dog new tricks.

Table of Contents

Introduction 9

Our Commitment to Training 18

The Goal of a Dog Trainer 21

How Our Training System Was Created .. 27

Dogs See In Pictures 37

Puppy Training 43

Potty Training... 61

10 Sins Of Dog Training 69

10 Virtues Of Dog Training............................... 81

Anxiety and Aggression.................................... 93

Dog Quiz 97

PAWS, for a Notable Quotable

"A goal is a dream with a deadline."

-NAPOLEON HILL
(The best-selling author of Think & Grow Rich.)

Want to open your own Make Your Dog Epic dog training business?
Learn how to have your own! Open one of the most affordable and turn-key dog training businesses on the planet at MakeYourDogEpic.com.

A NOTE FROM THE CREATOR OF THE MAKE YOUR DOG EPIC DOG TRAINING SYSTEM.

When you first start learning about dog training, sometimes it feels like the more you know, the less you know. There are thousands of dog trainers in America, all with different methods, training philosophies, training tools, and certifications. I have written this book from my experience having worked with thousands of dogs as a dog trainer, and from the teachings I have learned from Hollywood Dog trainers like Joel Silverman and Bryan Renfro, as well as trainers who changed my whole perspective on dog training like Tim Smith with 7F Dog Training, and others. Go to our website www.MakeYourDogEpic.com to see more information about our training method and philosophy. I understand there are many ways to train a dog, however, what we have done at Make Your Dog Epic is learn many different ways and methods of dog training and compressed it into our own transferable, teachable, repeatable, and scalable methodology we feel is the easiest way for both humans and dogs to understand. My passion is helping both you and your dog in the most repeatable and duplicatable way possible. I am honored you have put your trust in us to serve you and your dog. We do not take it for granted.

My goal is to provide you with the best dog training experience possible! As well as a method that is extremely easy to transfer to anyone in the family. We refer to our method as Focused Based Positive Reinforcement Training and Methodology. When you sign up for our 50 Cent lesson we will show you how we train your dog transparently and right in front of you, so you can see our dog training best-practices and systems first-hand. However, this book is meant to lay a foundation for dog training no matter what method you use.

Want to open your own Make Your Dog Epic dog training business? Learn how to have your own! Open one of the most affordable and turn-key dog training businesses on the planet at MakeYourDogEpic.com.

Our ultimate goal at Make Your Dog Epic is to give dogs a better life through world-class and transferable dog training. In our society, dogs that listen get more freedom to go out in public or even just interact with the family and friends of dog owners. A goal for a lot of people is off-leash freedom with their dog. So they can go to places like the beach, public parks, or hiking trails. However, regardless of what your dog training goals are, we will get you there. We've structured this book so you can read it out of sequence if you wish. Feel free to jump around while reading the book. However, reading it in order will offer you significant benefits. In order to emphasize certain key themes and ideas, we have repeated certain concepts in the book. We hope you enjoy this book and journey on your way to having an EPIC dog!

Our Mission: Obedience but NEVER at the expense of the dog's personality. If you have to crush your dog's spirit to get it to listen, what's the point?

When reading this book, remember you can be as strict or as lenient with any commands or training as you want. My goal as a dog trainer is to get you to your specific goals!

(**Disclaimer**: This book is for real dogs not robot dogs.)

Want to open your own Make Your Dog Epic dog training business?
Learn how to have your own! Open one of the most affordable and turn-key dog training businesses on the planet at MakeYourDogEpic.com.

Introduction

A NOTE FROM CO-FOUNDER, CLAY CLARK

I want to give this short book to all of our wonderful clients, locations, and hard-working owners because I believe it's important to be extremely transparent about how we train dogs and my proven philosophy of how we run our business.

Whether you're a client seeking our expertise, a dedicated Make Your Dog Epic employee in training, a committed Make Your Dog Epic owner, or simply an eager learner looking to dive into the world of dog training, know this: Our unwavering mission revolves around one singular goal-creating, well-behaved, joyful dogs alongside their equally joyful owners. No one dog is the same, and no one owner is the same. This is why we offer our first lesson for 50 cents. We want to figure out what it will take to get each dog to their owner's goals. The question I thought about throughout the process of creating this system is:

> ❓ *"What's the value in a dog's obedience, if it doesn't come with happiness?"*

Our goal is: "Obedience but NEVER at the expense of personality." There are many ways to train a dog and there is no regulatory body over dog training in the United States. It would be the equivalent of being a doctor, but not needing to go to school, or aspiring to be like a lawyer, but the Bar Exam being voluntary.

Then, even if you did take the Bar Exam, there is no governing body over it making sure they are meeting certain standards.

Want to open your own Make Your Dog Epic dog training business?
Learn how to have your own! Open one of the most affordable and turn-key dog training businesses on the planet at MakeYourDogEpic.com.

Basically, when it comes to dog training certifications and experience, doesn't mean anything. Because there is no governing body over certifications, they could've been doing it wrong for the last 20 years. Just because you have experience in something doesn't mean it's good experience. What matters is happy customers. We pride ourselves on having the happiest clients who leave raving reviews and testimonials about us. That's all that matters. As a trainer or licensee with Make Your Dog Epic, our #1 goal is happy dogs and happy clients!

In this short training guide, I teach our training standards and the workflow we actually use to run our business.

WHAT DOES CLAY CLARK DO?

Clay Clark helps clients and himself to scale and grow successful, sustainable and profitable businesses. See thousands of documented Clay Clark client success stories today at: https://www.thrivetimeshow.com/testimonials/

"Clay Clark has been recognized nationally by the White House as Oklahoma's Small Business Entrepreneur of the Year, and he still hasn't reached the sea-soned age of forty. He has learned to leverage his business acumen and now finds himself in multiple successful business partnerships.So I was not surprised at all when he set out to launch Thrive15.com – the place to get what you need to know to get you where you want to go. Those are his words. This book extends his winning talks beyond sold-out conferences to an audience of thousands morenation wide and around the world. And through Thrive15.com, he will open up passageways for others to live beyond the "just surviving" mentality. He celebrates success wherever it is found. He understands the hard work and dedication

---

Want to open your own Make Your Dog Epic dog training business? Learn how to have your own! Open one of the most affordable and turn-key dog training businesses on the planet at MakeYourDogEpic.com.

required. He really does admire Napoleon Hill and fills his life with Mr. Hill's actionable quotes. They are all through this book. As I look at Clay's success and his larger-than-life vision for his future, he is well on his way to emulating the man he so admires. And quite frankly, he is placing him in a similar position to be admired and quoted as his life and businesses continue to THRIVE. Oftentimes people offering advice simply trust that the mes-sage is understood and move on, but not Clay Clark. He is committed to being in your face for your success. Not afraid of repetitious conversation and in-your-face humor, he is committed to each reader getting the message and more importantly, implementing the action steps set forth in this book and those voiced at Thrive15.com.Embracing and implementing the action steps in his books and training. Clay Clark is obsessed with implementing the action steps around your "big idea." This man gets emotional over your business success – maximizing your talents and potential. He remembers his dorm-room start and fully celebrates yours. Quoting Clay, "My friend, as you can tell by now, running a successful business is about so much more than just having a 'big idea.'

Your BIG IDEA is important, but the overwhelming majority of what will make your business succeed or fail has little to do with the 'big idea itself and everything to do with the execution of the 'big idea.'" Clay Leaves us no doubt that action on our part matters. His life as well as his insightful consulting encounters become a clear window through which we can look and see what is possible in many of our lives if we are willing to put in the time and effort necessary to turn ideas into reality. Clay clearly points out that our "want to" becomes the driver of our actions or lack of actions.Yes, I could have failed had I not embraced the notion that execution of a plan matters. Clay is right. His life challenges us to not settle, but to THRIVE. In doing so, we place ourselves in a position to light the darkness for others. It is in our reach to others that we truly maximize

Want to open your own Make Your Dog Epic dog training business?
Learn how to have your own! Open one of the most affordable and turn-key dog training businesses on the planet at MakeYourDogEpic.com.

our existence on this planet. If I were still home in the Delta doing the same thing all those around me were doing, I seriously doubt if I would be able to light the pathway for myself or others. Today I am lighting the darkness as a businessman and writer, telling others what is possible for their lives. Clay's passionate plea for others to move beyond merely surviving comes from an honest place of caring. Why fail when you can THRIVE? Thank you, Clay, for not being afraid to step out beyond the ordinary and for inviting us along on your remarkable journey."

– Clifton L. Taulbert

(The first African American west of the Mississippi to found a bank, a Pulitzer-Prize Nominated and Best-selling Author, long-time Clay Clark mentor and the President of the Building Community Institute President & CEO)

I am the co-founder of five kids, the former "U.S. SBA Entrepreneur of the Year" for the State of Oklahoma, the founder of several multi-million dollar companies, and the host of the *Thrivetime Show* podcast, which has been number one overall on the iTunes business podcast charts 6 times. I have been a member of the *Forbes* Business Coach Council, an Amazon best-selling author and the host of the *Thrivetime Show*. Throughout my career I've co-founded / founded several successful businesses including:

- www.DJConnection.com
- www.EpicPhotos.com
- www.EITRLounge.com
- www.MakeYourLifeEpic.com
- Party Perfect (Which was purchased by Party Pro Rentals)
- TipTopK9 Franchising (I did not start TipTopK9 Dog Training, I co-founded TipTopK9 Franchising)

Want to open your own Make Your Dog Epic dog training business? Learn how to have your own! Open one of the most affordable and turn-key dog training businesses on the planet at MakeYourDogEpic.com.

Introduction

» www.Thrive15.com
   (The interactive, online entrepreneurship school)
» The Tulsa Bridal Association Wedding Show

Throughout my career, I have been featured in *Fast Company*, *Bloomberg*, *Forbes*, *Entrepreneur Magazine*, *PandoDaily*, and numerous other publications. I've been the speaker and consultant of choice for top brands throughout the country including: Hewlett Packard, Maytag University, Valspar Paint, and O'Reilly's Auto Parts. I'm also the co-founder of 5 children, the proud owner of thousands of trees, dozens of chickens, 13 cats, and one dog by the name of "Davis".

Since launching my ThrivetimeShow.com Podcast, the podcast has hit the top of the iTunes podcast charts 6 times and has featured interviews with hundreds of super successful entrepreneurs including those listed below and more:

8x *New York Times* Best-Selling Author and Leadership Expert, John Maxwell

Celebrity Chef, Entrepreneur, and *New York Times* Best-Selling Author, Wolfgang Puck

Legendary Former Key Apple Employee-Turned-Venture Capitalist, Best Selling Author, Guy Kawasaki

New York Times Best-Selling Co-Author of "Rich Dad Poor Dad", Sharon Lechter

Senior pastor of the largest church in America with over 100,000 weekly attendees (Lifechurch.tv), Craig Groeschel

One of America's most trusted financial experts who has written nine consecutive *New York Times* bestsellers with over 7 million books in print, David Bach

Legendary Conservative Strategist, Roger Stone

NBA Hall of Famer, David Robinson
(2x NBA Champion, 2-time Gold Medal Winner)

Want to open your own Make Your Dog Epic dog training business?
Learn how to have your own! Open one of the most affordable and turn-key dog training businesses on the planet at MakeYourDogEpic.com.

Make Your Dog Epic

Senior Editor for *Forbes* and 3x Best-Selling Author, Zack O'Malley Greenburg

Most Downloaded Business Podcaster of All-Time (EOFire.com), John Lee Dumas

The 25th U.S. National Security Advisor, and Retired U.S. Army General, Michael Flynn

New York Times Best-Selling Author of "Purple Cow", and former *Yahoo!* Vice President of Marketing, Seth Godin

Co-Founder of the 700+ Employee Advertising Company (AdRoll), Adam Berke

Emmy Award-Winning Producer of the *Today Show* and *New York Times* Best-Selling Author of "Sh*tty Moms", Mary Ann Zoellner

New York Times Best-Selling Author of "Contagious: Why Things Catch On" and *Wharton* Business Professor, Jonah Berger

New York Times Best-Selling Author of "Made to Stick" and *Duke University* Professor, Dan Heath

International Best-Selling Author of "In Search of Excellence", Tom Peters

NBA Player and Coach, Muggsy Bogues (Shortest player to ever play in the league)

NFL Running Back, Rashad Jennings (and Winner of *Dancing with the Stars*)

Lee Cockerell (The former Executive Vice President of Walt Disney World, who once managed 40,000 employees)

Michael Levine (PR consultant of choice for Michael Jackson, Prince, Nike, Charlton Heston, Nancy Kerrigan, etc.)

Billboard Contemporary Christian Top 40 Recording Artist, Colton Dixon

Conservative Talk Pundit, Frequent *Fox News* Contributor, Political Commentator, and Best-Selling Author, Ben Shapiro

Want to open your own Make Your Dog Epic dog training business? Learn how to have your own! Open one of the most affordable and turn-key dog training businesses on the planet at MakeYourDogEpic.com.

See additional guests at: ThrivetimeShow.com

Make Your Life Epic is a business consulting practice where I and my team coach 160 business owners every month in many different industries. The systems we recommend at Make Your Dog Epic are the same systems used in all industries to make them successful.

"When you WOW your clients they will refer you close to now." - Clay Clark

Do you own a business? Well, I have a long track record of helping people to grow businesses using best-practice systems, processes, checklists, strategies, and moves I use.

Thousands of our client success stories can be found at: www.ThrivetimeShow.com. So, what is Make Your Life Epic? Make Your Life Epic is a best-practice business growth consulting company where I and my team coach 160 business owners in many different industries. The systems we use at Make Your Dog Epic are the same proven systems I teach our clients to make them successful.

PAWS, for a Fun Fact

A dog can smell anywhere from 10,000 to 100,000X better than the average human. The part of the brain dedicated to smell is 40X larger in dogs than in humans.

- MentalFloss.com

Want to open your own Make Your Dog Epic dog training business?
Learn how to have your own! Open one of the most affordable and turn-key dog training businesses on the planet at MakeYourDogEpic.com.

READ CLAY CLARK'S BOOK(S):

Download Clay Clark's Books for Free at:
https://www.ThrivetimeShow.com/free-resources

CLAY IS THE AUTHOR OF 20+ BOOKS INCLUDING:

A MILLIONAIRE'S GUIDE TO BECOMING SUSTAINABLY RICH
The World's Best Business Growth & Consulting Book: Business Growth Strategies from the World's Best Business Coach.

F6 JOURNAL
Meta Thrive Time Journal.

BOOM
The 14 Proven Steps to Business Success.

WHEEL OF WEALTH
An Entrepreneur's Action Guide.

JACKASSARY
Jackassery will serve as a beacon of light for other entrepreneurs that are looking to avoid troublesome employees and difficult situations. This is real. This is raw. This is unfiltered entrepreneurship.

THE ENTREPRENEUR'S DRAGON ENERGY
The Mindset Kanye, Trump and You Need to Succeed.

MAKE YOUR LIFE EPIC
Clay shares his journey and struggle from the dorm room to the board room during his raw and action-packed story of how he built DJConnection.com.

THRIVE
How to Take Control of Your Destiny and Move Beyond Surviving... Now!

THE ART OF GETTING THINGS DONE
Time-tested Super moves that you can use to create both the time freedom and financial freedom that most people only dream about.

SALES DOMINATION
Clay Clark is a master of selling and now he wants to teach you his proven processes, scalable systems and sales mastery moves in a humorous and practical way.

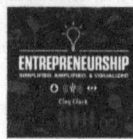
ENTREPRENEURSHIP: SIMPLIFIED, AMPLIFIED, & VISUALIZED
Throughout my career, I have been blessed to achieve tremendous success both as an entrepreneur and as a podcast host.

WILL NOT WORK FOR FOOD
9 Big Ideas for Effectively Managing Your Business in an Increasingly Dumb, Distracted & Dishonest America.

HOW TO REPEL FRIENDS AND NOT INFLUENCE PEOPLE
The epic whale of a tale featuring America's self proclaimed most humble male.

DON'T LET YOUR EMPLOYEES HOLD YOU HOSTAGE
This candid book shares how to avoid being held hostage by employees.

IT'S NOT LONELY AT THE TOP
15 Keys to achieving a successful, peaceful, and drama-free life. (3/4 of this book is handwritten by Clay Clark, himself).

TRADE-UPS
Learn how to design and live the life you love, how to find and create the time needed to get things done in a world filled with endless digital distractions, and more!

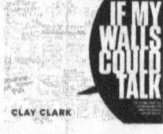
IF MY WALLS COULD TALK
The Notes, Quotes, & Epiphanies I've Written On Clay's Office Walls. (Hardcover).

SEARCH ENGINE DOMINATION
Learn the Proven System We've Used to Earn Millions.

PODCAST DOMINATION 101
This book will show you how to prepare, record, launch, and begin generating income from your podcast, all from your home studio!

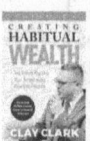
CREATING HABITUAL WEALTH
Are you looking for a proven and practical plan for achieving financial freedom? In this millionaire's guide, Clay Clark teaches the specific steps that you need to take in order to create habitual wealth.

Want to open your own Make Your Dog Epic dog training business? Learn how to have your own! Open one of the most affordable and turn-key dog training businesses on the planet at MakeYourDogEpic.com.

PAWS, for a Fun Fact

According to Forbes, dogs are the most popular pet in the United States with 65.1 million U.S. households owning dogs. Approximately 49.5% of American households own a dog.

- Forbes
(January 25, 2024.)

Want to open your own Make Your Dog Epic dog training business?
Learn how to have your own! Open one of the most affordable and turn-key dog training businesses on the planet at MakeYourDogEpic.com.

Our Commitment to Training

Our commitment is that we will be there for you and your dog even after you've completed your tailored dog training package. We train many dogs that have trained with other trainers, however, those who train with us never train anywhere else. Not necessarily because we are superior trainers, but because we will be there for the rest of your dog's life! With numerous dog trainers, training tools, methods, myths, and misconceptions out there, we are honored that you chose us to embark on this journey with you and your pup.

We will help you and your dog to achieve your specific goals. We understand that all dogs are unique, and everyone has distinct objectives with their pup. Whatever those goals may be, we will guide you and your dog down the path, until you reach them. We offer a money-back guarantee and we will NEVER shift blame to you if the training doesn't work. It will always be our responsibility!

No matter which training program you choose with us, group classes are included and you get lifetime phone support. That's because we want to be there for the entirety of your dog's life! Let's make your dog EPIC!

CLAY CLARK
Founder of
MakeYourDogEpic.com

J.T. LAWSON
Owner & Lead Trainer
MakeYourDogEpic.com
OKLAHOMA LOCATIONS

Want to open your own Make Your Dog Epic dog training business? Learn how to have your own! Open one of the most affordable and turn-key dog training businesses on the planet at MakeYourDogEpic.com.

Our Commitment to Training

PAWS,
for a Fun Fact

"We all get good ideas at seminars and from books and business-building gurus. The problem is that most companies do not know how to identify and adapt the best ideas to their businesses. Implementation, not ideas, is the key to real success."

- CHET HOMES
(The best-selling author of "The Ultimate Sales Machine", and legendary business growth consultant.)

Want to open your own Make Your Dog Epic dog training business?
Learn how to have your own! Open one of the most affordable and turn-key dog training businesses on the planet at MakeYourDogEpic.com.

PAWS, for a Notable Quotable

"At Make Your Dog Epic, we believe that the service, products, and solutions that we provide should be so good that you'll want to work with us. Having grown thousands of businesses, I believe that anyone teaching highly manipulative sales techniques, whether they have a beard and an eye patch or not, is a modern pirate and a sick, twisted freak. It does not matter to me whether someone is suffering from "little-king" syndrome or they are just a timid, cowardly, and weak force individual. Any sales person who actually devotes time every week to learn and train himself and his team how to implement highly manipulative and high-pressure sales techniques is not someone with whom I would do business."

CLAY CLARK

Want to open your own Make Your Dog Epic dog training business? Learn how to have your own! Open one of the most affordable and turn-key dog training businesses on the planet at MakeYourDogEpic.com.

CHAPTER 1
The Goal of a Dog Trainer

JOKE TIME
Q: What do you call a Frozen Dog?
A: Pupsicle

I am writing this section from the heart because it genuinely hurts me that many dog trainers get this very wrong. Most dog trainers and dog training companies, I believe, started out with good intentions, but they lose their way somewhere down the road.

> "YOU CAN NOT ONLY IMPROVE THE LIFE OF THE DOG THROUGH DOG TRAINING BUT YOU CAN LITERALLY SAVE DOGS' LIVES THROUGH DOG TRAINING."

They started out with a passion for dogs. They love dogs, they care for dogs, they want the absolute best for them. Next, they start learning as much as they can, so they watch YouTube videos of training and try a couple of things. They possibly even bought a couple of dog training books or attended seminars. They start having success and get infatuated with the dog training realm. They start training other people's dogs or get a job as a dog trainer. They get really good, and they have a deep passion for dogs and people. They understand that behavioral issues are one of the top reasons dogs are surrendered to shelters. You can not only improve the life of the dog through dog training but you can literally save dogs' lives through dog training. My dog Riley is a shelter dog I got from the Williamson County Animal Shelter. She was their longest-stay there. She was there for over 6 months when I saw her. The whole time she was on the verge of being euthanized because of her behavior issues. She was very kennel aggressive and dog-aggressive. She is decent when it comes to people unless it's a crowd of kids or a grown man that's holding something resembling a pole or stick. She also has such a high toy drive that when people would come to visit her, she only cared about the toy instead of the new people. Not to mention, she was in a shelter in Alabama then surrendered to a shelter in Clarksville Tennessee, then she was given to Williamson County shelter as a stray. Needless to say, she has been through a lot. I got her when she was already 4 years old.

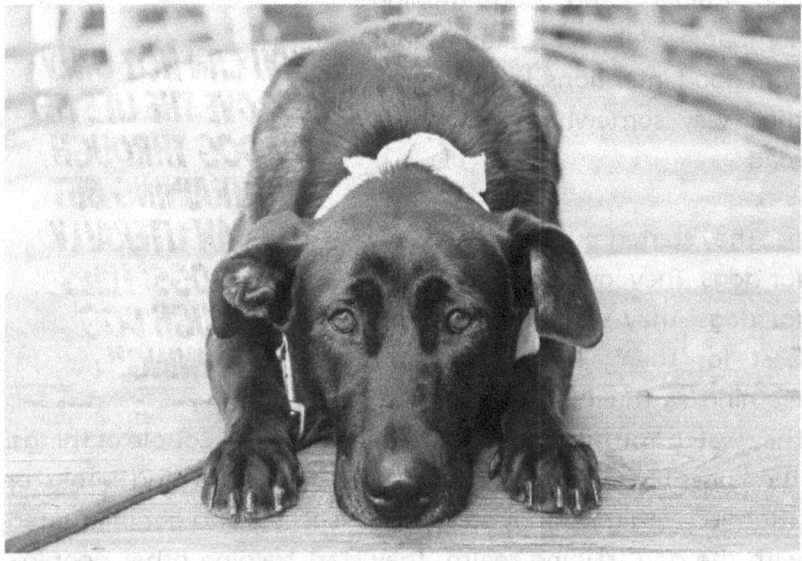

When I got her, she would not 'COME' no matter what anyone said or how loud they said it. She would jump on everyone, and she would immediately get aggressive around new dogs. She would resource guard. All these reasons are why she kept getting

Want to open your own Make Your Dog Epic dog training business? Learn how to have your own! Open one of the most affordable and turn-key dog training businesses on the planet at MakeYourDogEpic.com.

put back in shelters and not adopted. I was genuinely able to save her life through dog training. She does everything Achilles

does now. I still can't bring her to events because she gets overwhelmed in large crowds. However, she can now have a great life!

She gets off-leash freedom to play fetch, explore, play with Achilles, and jump in ponds. That is such a rewarding thing.

Here she is on a fire hydrant!

I give this story not to brag but to showcase that the goal of a dog trainer should be to SERVE. Serve the owner and the dog. I believe that is how most dog trainers start out. At some point down the line, it turns into wanting to be better than other dog trainers, speaking negatively about other dog trainers and owners, and using high-pressure sales tactics. They start worrying about comparing their own personal dog to other dog trainers' dogs and tearing them down instead of appreciating them for helping others.

Want to open your own Make Your Dog Epic dog training business?
Learn how to have your own! Open one of the most affordable and turn-key dog training businesses on the planet at MakeYourDogEpic.com.

For example, we recently did a home show, and there was another dog training company there. We had multiple people coming over to us saying they were talking badly about our company. They were more interested in talking badly about us than they were in serving their customers. No matter what realm of business you are in, you shouldn't have to talk badly about your competition to be able to get new customers. No matter how you train — not every single person in the world is going to like it, so you should be happy when someone finds a different trainer. The goal is happy dogs and clients. If we are booked out, we will recommend other trainers in town because we want them to find the help they need.

Trainers also have issues pushing their goals onto their clients. For example, I have trained and shadowed trainers that will sell a high-end package to a client that teaches the dog super long stays, 'COME' perfectly centered up and look the owner in the eye, 'HEEL OFF LEASH' and a bunch of other stuff for a 4-week boot camp. After the sales lesson, I asked, "Their biggest issues were jumping on people and barking. Wouldn't the cheaper package fix all these issues?" No exaggeration, they said, "Yeah, but did you see their cars? They can afford it." Every single sales lesson he had, he wouldn't actually listen to their problems; he would just try to get as much money out of them as possible. Or they think all dogs should be trained to their version of perfection and anything else is not acceptable. If any trainer believes differently, they will absolutely verbally bash them or turn into a keyboard warrior and bash them online.

> **PRO TIP:**
> **MONEY IS AN AMPLIFIER. IF YOU ARE A PIECE OF CRAP BEFORE YOU MAKE A LOT OF MONEY, IT WILL JUST TURN YOU INTO A BIGGER PIECE OF CRAP. BE CAREFUL WHO YOU TEACH TO MAKE MONEY BECAUSE YOU'RE GOING TO AMPLIFY THEIR CHARACTER.**

Want to open your own Make Your Dog Epic dog training business? Learn how to have your own! Open one of the most affordable and turn-key dog training businesses on the planet at MakeYourDogEpic.com.

I'm leaving names out of it because I don't believe in tearing down other trainers. But, I use this to hopefully educate new trainers on what NOT to do. The same trainer that I shadowed would use super dirty sales moves. I'll explain one to you. This s the move he taught all of his team to do. If a new customer says, "Well, I need to think about it or, I can't afford the package."— whatever the cost is. We will use $2,000 as an example. The response his team is supposed to say in a slow and low voice, "ahh ok, got it. Your dog currently doesn't 'COME' on command, which means they are probably going to get out the front door again. Next time, the chances are pretty high that it will get hit by a car. Is it fair to say your dog's life is worth less to you than $2,000?" He would guilt-trip them into buying packages, and a rule for their salespeople is that they cannot leave the lesson unless they get a 100% yes or a 100% no. They will sit in your house forever if all you do is say, "I have to think about it".

Make sure you don't forget your reason for starting to train dogs. Don't forget to serve people. Don't become a weak, feeble-minded little king who gets to their goals at the expense of others. Don't tear other people down to build yourself up. You should carry yourself with confidence but also be humble and remember your beginnings. Never screw over the people who put you on their back and helped you get to the top of the mountain, because if you do, it's a long way down. Strive for your goals but don't do it at the expense of others. Or simply put in the dog training world "don't bite the hand that feeds you". Even dogs understand that.

As a dog trainer, you're not only effecting the lives of dogs but the human's life as well. Think about how incredibly blessed you are to be able to do a job that's a paid hobby. You're paid to have fun and change lives. Keep that at the front of your mind at all times.

Want to open your own Make Your Dog Epic dog training business?
Learn how to have your own! Open one of the most affordable and turn-key dog training businesses on the planet at MakeYourDogEpic.com.

PAWS, for a Notable Quotable

"You will never reach your destination if you stop and throw stones at every dog that barks."

-WINSTON S. CHURCHILL

(The Prime Minister of the United Kingdom from 1940 to 1945 who defiantly stood up alone against Adolf Hitler and the Nazi party's quest to take over the world and to remove the Jewish people from the planet Earth.)

Want to open your own Make Your Dog Epic dog training business? Learn how to have your own! Open one of the most affordable and turn-key dog training businesses on the planet at MakeYourDogEpic.com.

CHAPTER 2

How Our Training System Was Created

> THIS CHAPTER IS THE ABBREVIATED VERSION OF OUR WEBSITE PAGE. TO VIEW MORE, VISIT MAKEYOURDOGEPIC.COM. WE HAVE VIDEOS AS WELL AS PODCASTS THERE.

JOKE TIME

Q: What happens when you cross a dog with a lion?
A: You won't be getting any mail, that's for sure.

I have come up with my own dog training system after years of training and learning from the best dog trainers in the industry. One of my strengths as a person is being coachable. When I go to learn from a trainer I brain dump all of the preconceptions I have about dog training. I try to be a sponge and soak up all of the knowledge they have to offer. I will constantly be on a journey to learn all there is about dog training. I have traveled the United States learning from some of the best trainers there are. With one goal in mind: soak up knowledge so I can then create a dog training system that not only gets the best results but is also the easiest for the dog and client to understand.

With our mission in mind, "Obedience but never at the expense of personality", I went on my journey. Most people don't know but there is no governing body over dog training, so the range of training varies so much.

This includes:

- Positive reinforcement training
- Clicker Training
- Model Training
- Mirror Training
- Compulsion training
- Alpha Dog Theory
- Operant Conditioning
- Discriminated Operant
- Active Avoidance
- Discriminated Omission
- Passive Avoidance
- Classical conditioning
- Fear conditioning
- Taste Aversion

There are so many different training methods. Not only that, but you have the different training tools that coincide with the methods. Such as:

- Flat collar
- Choke chains
- Martingale collar
- Prong collar
- Gentle Leader
- Pinch Collar
- Haltis
- Harnesses
- Heeling sticks
- Treats
- All the different kind of treats
- Clickers
- Target sticks
- Shock collars
- E-collars
- Whistles
- All the different leashes

Want to open your own Make Your Dog Epic dog training business? Learn how to have your own! Open one of the most affordable and turn-key dog training businesses on the planet at MakeYourDogEpic.com.

The list goes on and on. When first learning, it can be very confusing. I thought to myself while training, there has to be a better way. I found a trainer named Tim Smith, and his 7F

method of dog training is a foundational aspect of our training. I learned and continue to learn so much from Tim Smith. When I went out and learned from him, the information I gained GREATLY outweighed the cost of paying to learn from him. His underlying foundation in life and dog training is "Serving." When you are going through life, working with dogs, working with clients, in all you do

"OUR MISSION: OBEDIENCE, BUT NEVER AT THE EXPENSE OF THE DOG'S PERSONALITY!"

you should be serving and through that give glory to God and be an Advocate for Christ. Here are a couple of pictures from my time training with him. He also taught me and my dog Achilles "Retrieve". If you ever see me with one of my dogs on a baseball field, I owe it to Tim Smith for teaching me how to teach it. He also thought it would be fun for me to take a bite from one of the dogs they were working with. I told them I wasn't scared but my face obviously tell you I lied HAH!

On our website is a fun video where we went to the Las Vegas strip and talked to people about different dog training techniques. We had a great time showing them all of Achille's tricks.

I have gained experience from having worked with thousands of dogs as a dog trainer, and from the teachings I have learned from Hollywood Dog trainers like Joel Silverman and Bryan Renfro, as well as trainers who changed my whole perspective on dog training like Tim Smith with 7F Dog Training and others. Go to our website www.MakeYourDogEpic.com to see more information about our training method and philosophy. I understand there are many ways to train a dog, however what we have done at Make Your Dog Epic is learn many different ways and methods of dog training and have compressed it into our own transferable, teachable, repeatable and scalable methodology that we feel is the easiest way for both humans and dogs to understand. My passion is helping both you and your dog in the most repeatable and duplicatable way possible.

My goal is to provide you with the best dog training experience possible that is the easiest to transfer to anyone in the family. We refer to our method as Focused Based Positive Reinforcement Training and Methodology. When you sign up for our 50 cent lesson we will show you how we train your dog transparently, and right in front of you so that you can see our dog training best-practices and systems first-hand. However, this book is meant to lay a foundation for Dog Training no matter what method you use. Our ultimate goal at Make Your Dog Epic is to give dogs a better life through world-class and transferable dog training. In our society dogs that listen get more freedom to go out in public or even just interact with the family and friends of dog owners. Dog owners that have a well-behaved and

Want to open your own Make Your Dog Epic dog training business?
Learn how to have your own! Open one of the most affordable and turn-key dog training businesses on the planet at MakeYourDogEpic.com.

well-trained dog want to introduce their dogs to people! However, regardless of what your dog training goals are, we will get you there. We've structured this book so you can read it out of sequence if you wish. Feel free to jump around while reading the book. However, reading it in order will offer you significant benefits. In order to emphasize certain key themes and ideas we have repeated certain concepts in the book. We hope you enjoy this book and journey on your way to having an EPIC dog!

Our Mission: Obedience, but NEVER at the expense of the dog's personality. If you have to crush your dog's spirit to get it to listen, what's the point?

I also went to learn from Joel Silverman and Bryan Renfro at a dog training conference called "Dog Training For Film & TV Course" I learned a lot during my time training with them! It was much more than just dog training! I talked to them about the conference in the interviews below! Listen to find out more!

This is a photo of me with Celebrity Dog Trainers Joel Silverman and Bryan Renfro

Want to open your own Make Your Dog Epic dog training business?
Learn how to have your own! Open one of the most affordable and turn-key dog training businesses on the planet at MakeYourDogEpic.com.

Who Is Joel Silverman?

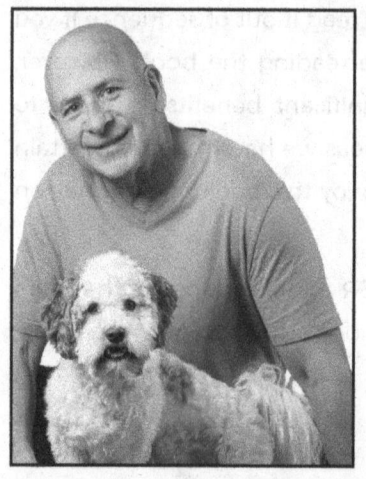

The legendary dog trainer Joel Silverman was born and raised in Southern California. And at the very young age of just 13 years old, he trained his family dog, which was the first animal he ever trained. Shadow. During this period of celebrity dog trainer Joel Silverman's life, both he and his family decided to spend their summer vacations in beautiful San Diego, California, which is in southern California. During their vacation time spent together in San Diego, California the family would often visit SeaWorld. After spending multiple summers watching professional trainers riding orcas, Joel Silverman became very interested in whales and the whale trainers.

At just 16 years old, Joel Silverman got hired to be a trash collector at SeaWorld. However, after investing years of his time into assisting the trainers, Joel Silverman got hired as an actual trainer to work at the world-famous SeaWorld. Joel began training both Pacific and Atlantic bottle-nosed dolphins and California sea lions. However, eventually and after years and years of diligence and training, Joel Silverman became a trainer of orcas at SeaWorld!!!

In 1983, Joel Silverman began to change his focus to training the celebrity animals that people see when they watch movies, TV, film and commercials. In fact during the years of 1988 to 1992, Joel Silverman became the trainer for Dreyfuss from the TV series Empty nest. Then in 1989, Joel Silverman went on to host and create his first

Want to open your own Make Your Dog Epic dog training business? Learn how to have your own! Open one of the most affordable and turn-key dog training businesses on the planet at MakeYourDogEpic.com.

dog training video called Joel Silverman's Hollywood Dog Training Program. This dog training video went on to sell more than 300,000 videos!!! Then 10 years later, in 1999, Joel hosted his first TV series called "GOOD DOG U" which aired on animal planet for a decade from 1999-2009.

Learn More About Joel Silverman Today At:

www.JoelSilverman.net

BUY JOEL SILVERMAN'S BOOKS TODAY:

  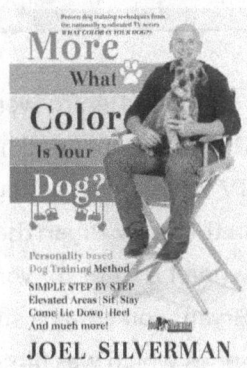

RITUALS

Understanding how, why, and when to either motivate or eliminate your dogs natural behaviors

Hardcover – July 15th, 2020

WHAT COLOR IS YOUR DOG?

Train Your Dog Based on His Personality "Color" (Kennel Club Books)

Hardcover – June 16, 2009

MORE WHAT COLOR IS YOUR DOG?

Understanding how, why, and when to either motivate or eliminate your dogs natural behaviors

Paperback – September 30, 2015

Want to open your own Make Your Dog Epic dog training business?
Learn how to have your own! Open one of the most affordable and turn-key dog training businesses on the planet at MakeYourDogEpic.com.

Bryan Renfro

Bryan Renfro became known as one of the top dog trainers in all of Hollywood in the 1980s and 1990s. Bryan Renfro became well known and respected within the animal training industry for performing at the Animal Actors Stage at Universal Studios in the 1970s and 1980s where he personally trained Fred the Cockatoo from the Baretta TV series.

Bryan Renfro went on to train Bandit from Little House on the Prairie TV series and he even trained Boomer from the Here's Boomer TV series. Bryan actually performed with the animals he was training in the show. Bryan then went on to work on both sides of the camera when he went to work on the Rin-Tin-Tin TV series as a dog trainer. Bryan worked as a stuntman from 1988-1993 on the Rin-Tin-Tin TV series which was filmed up north in Toronto, California.

Learn More About Bryan Renfro Today At:
www.JoelSilverman.net/Bryan-Renfro/

BUY BRYAN RENFRO'S BOOK TODAY:

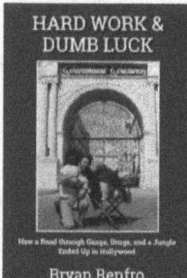

HARD WORK & DUMB LUCK:

How a Road through Gangs, Drugs, and a Jungle Ended Up in Hollywood

March 9th, 2021

Want to open your own Make Your Dog Epic dog training business? Learn how to have your own! Open one of the most affordable and turn-key dog training businesses on the planet at MakeYourDogEpic.com.

How Our Training System Was Created

PAWS, for a Fun Fact

Dogs sweat through their paws instead of their armpits.

Want to open your own Make Your Dog Epic dog training business?
Learn how to have your own! Open one of the most affordable and turnkey dog training businesses on the planet at MakeYourDogEpic.com.

PAWS, for a Notable Quotable

"No one lives long enough to learn everything they need to learn starting from scratch. To be successful, we absolutely, positively have to find people who have already paid the price to learn the things that we need to learn to achieve our goals."

BRIAN TRACY
(Best-Selling author, international speaker, sales trainer and business growth consultant)

CHAPTER 3
Dogs See In Pictures

JOKE TIME
Q: Where should you go if your dog is missing?
A: The lost and hound!

I want to start with this chapter because if you understand this concept, you automatically become a better dog trainer no matter what method of dog training you choose to use. You will also become a better dog owner when you understand that dogs see in pictures. Dogs see in 'pictures', and they don't think rationally like you and I do. You should constantly keep this idea in your mind while engaged in dog training. The easiest way to explain this is to provide you with a couple of examples. First, is a common example in the dog training world. The mailman.

EXAMPLE NUMBER 1:
THE MAILMAN

The mailman comes to the door, the dog barks, and then the mailman leaves. In the dog's head, it thinks, "Wait a second, did I just do that?" Then, it happens again, and the dog thinks, "Oh, I did do that, awesome." Then it happens repeatedly, and every time it occurs, it seems to worsen. The dog starts to believe it just saved everyone in the house, the whole world, and is an honorary member of the Avengers now!

Want to open your own Make Your Dog Epic dog training business?
Learn how to have your own! Open one of the most affordable and turn-key dog training businesses on the planet at MakeYourDogEpic.com.

People typically use either positive or negative reinforcement in response to this behavior. Most opt for negative reinforcement because constant barking can be very annoying. It is also most people's default method of training. They may have read somewhere that they need to assert dominance in the household in order to have a well-behaved dog. Typically, they use dog training tools such as a prong collar, shock collar, fly swatter, choke chain, newspaper, squirt bottle, dad voice, etc.

Let's take the shock collar, for instance. When the mailman arrives and the dog barks, some people light the dog up with a shock collar. The dog is going to interpret this in one of two ways: either it understands and calms down, thinking, "Alright, I just need to chill out," or, more likely, because dogs see things in pictures and they do not think rationally, the dog associates the arrival of the mailman with its owner's anger and the shock from the collar. Now you have one or two outcomes from that. Either it gets worse and the dog starts barking louder, sooner, and more viscously, or the other outcome is the dog listens, but at the expense of the dog's personality, which is NEVER the goal.

EXAMPLE NUMBER 2: DOGS GOING ON A WALK

When you're going on a walk and you see a dog, your dog growls a little bit. The other dog leaves, and in your dog's head, it thinks, "That dog just left because I growled, and now I've saved mom, the whole world, and I'm part of the Avengers!" Then this scenario repeats over and over, resulting in win after win. People typically resort to some form of either negative or positive reinforcement.

Want to open your own Make Your Dog Epic dog training business? Learn how to have your own! Open one of the most affordable and turn-key dog training businesses on the planet at MakeYourDogEpic.com.

Most positive reinforcement trainers suggest a solution for this. You should get in front of the dog and redirect its attention to you. Then, when its attention is on you, you reward it. However, technically, you're rewarding bad behavior because the dog barks and you give it a treat. Even if your timing is perfect, your dog still associates barking at other dogs with getting a treat. This method might result in a reduction in constant barking and growling, but it doesn't entirely eliminate the behavior. Now, instead of just barking, it will bark, and then while barking, it will look at mom for a treat. Now, you need to have treats on you at all times, and your dog can never have a full stomach or they won't want treats, and the treats have to be super high value to overcome whatever the distraction level is.

Now, let's use the same example of going on a walk, but let's use a prong collar example. You have a trainer using a prong collar on the dog. Let's say the trainer does everything perfectly. He will turn and "pop" the dog hard enough to correct the dog. So now the dog walks perfectly for the trainer. This is very hard to transfer to clients, because now the trainer has to teach the client to have perfect timing. Also, maybe someone in the family doesn't have the strength or heart to use the prong collar. Well, now you're in a situation where the trainer will blame you for the training not working. Also, prong collars only work if you are attached to the dog with a leash. If you have no leash, you have no "authority".

*To see how we fix this issue, skip down to the anxiety and aggression chapter of the book.

First Picture: If you say 'COME' to the dog, and every time you make the dog come into the 'HEEL' position on your side. The dog sees in that 'picture' so then training it to come in straight and look at you is a completely different picture for the dog. Maybe you are teaching 'PLACE'. Well, it typically takes teaching place on 10 different spots before your dog will start to associate any elevated boundary as place.

Second Picture: If you teach, 'COME' and 'SIT' in front of you. But then while you're walking away you say come and the dog is allowed to run past you. You are mixing two different pictures with one command.

First picture: move towards me and you must sit in front of me

Second picture: move towards me, but you can do whatever you want.

When you do this and you're using the same command for both pictures, the first picture starts to get really blurry for the dog, and they don't know how to handle it. The solution is to label the second picture "let's go", and it can be as ugly as it needs to be. But you want to be strict on that first command because 'COME' is the command that's going to save the dog's life if it starts running into a street, or if you're hiking and there is a stray animal. 'COME' needs to mean you come and sit close enough to me that I can touch you without moving my feet, preferably touching me.

Dogs See In Pictures

PAWS,
for a Fun Fact

The average dog's mental age is equivalent to that of a two-and-a-half year old child judging by the number of words, signs, and signals the dog can understand.

- SafariVet.com

Want to open your own Make Your Dog Epic dog training business?
Learn how to have your own! Open one of the most affordable and turn-key dog training businesses on the planet at MakeYourDogEpic.com.

PAWS, for a Notable Quotable

"I've been screwed, I've had millions of dollars embezzled from me, and I've had ungrateful partners push me out of their businesses after I've helped them to grow their business by 18x without apology, simply to increase their income. At the end of the day, we must all choose to become bitter or better, or over time we will become so cold that we should wear a sweater."

-CLAY CLARK

(6X iTunes chart-topping podcast host and the co-creator of five human kids.)

Want to open your own Make Your Dog Epic dog training business? Learn how to have your own! Open one of the most affordable and turn-key dog training businesses on the planet at MakeYourDogEpic.com.

CHAPTER 4
Puppy Training

JOKE TIME
Q: Why do dogs float?
A: Because they're good buoys!

This chapter is primarily for people who want to start a good foundation with their puppies. This chapter of the book is filled with extra tips and tricks you can use before training with us. You could think of these tips and tricks as "hacks" to use before we start training your fur baby. Also, tips if you're thinking about getting a dog or how to find a good veterinarian near you, etc. This doesn't encompass all things puppies, but it's a good start. Your Make Your Dog Epic trainer can answer any specific questions you have!

KENNEL TRAINING

This topic is typically emotionally hard on dog owners. At Make Your Dog Epic, we do not use kennels as punishment— EVER. We use it as a training tool and a "den" for dogs. When it comes to kennel training, you can either do fast or slow. The choice is yours on what you feel like is the best option for your dog. There is no correct method. I tend to lean towards doing it fast with all my dogs unless I have an extremely anxious dog. Now you might be thinking, "I NEVER plan on putting my dog in a kennel. So I don't need to kennel train them." I understand, however, there are going to be times when you have no choice but to put your dog in a kennel. If that happens and your dog isn't kennel-trained, it is going to make it EXTREMELY tough for the dog. Here are some examples:

1. If you have to leave your dog at the veterinarian.
2. If you have to board your dog somewhere.
3. Potty training.
4. If you have them in a kennel while traveling in the car.
5. If they have to fly on an airplane.
6. If they need to be in a kennel at a hotel room.
7. If your dog gets injured and the veterinarian says you need to keep your dog in a kennel so it doesn't reinjure itself.
8. If you leave your dog at the groomers.

The examples can go on and on, but you get the point. Your dog is going to live a very long life. Thus, the chances of it never needing to be in a kennel is extremely low. So, if you don't want the first time kennel training your dog to be a traumatic time for it, I fully suggest you kennel train your dog early on in its life.

Here is how you get them to like their kennel. You can feed them inside the kennel with the door shut. They get 15 minutes to eat. If they don't eat, then the food goes back up, and they don't see it until their next time to eat. You might have to do this 3 or 4 times. The reason you're doing this is because we are teaching the dog to control their emotions and self-regulate their anxiety. The first couple times they might not eat. But, eventually they will think to themselves "I hate being in this kennel... However, I'm starving." They will take a metaphorical deep breath, relax, and start to eat. In return, this will over time teach them that when they feel like this, they need to take that deep breath. It will teach them to regulate their emotions.

You may also put them in the kennel randomly throughout the day for 30 seconds, 3 minutes, 10 min, etc., not just when you are going to leave the house for hours. That way your pup doesn't think they are going to be in the kennel for hours anytime they are put in it.

You don't want anything in the kennel the dog can chew up. Only put toys in the kennel that are not a choking hazard for the dog. Freedom is earned, not given, so if you want to put a blanket in the bottom that's fine. This is how you do it. You need to put the blanket in there for a couple minutes, and come back and check if it's chewed up. If you see that it's chewed up, you need to take it out and the dog loses blanket privileges. If it's not chewed up, then leave the blanket in for a little longer, and progressively extend the time. There are a LOT of dogs who don't get anything allowed in their kennel. This is normal, so don't be discouraged if you can't leave stuff in there. I honestly suggest people don't put anything in the kennel because we want it to be a place the dog can relax and shut its brain off. However, I know many people are going to put things in the kennel anyway, so I might as well tell you how to do it safely.

The dog "liking" their kennel and the dog going into the kennel everytime you ask are completely different things. You can work on teaching your dog to like the kennel. Our team will teach "kennel" and teach your dog to go there the first time you ask.

PLAY BITING

Most dogs will grow out of this phase by the age of 5 to 7 months old. The ease of fixing this issue usually depends on the specific breed of the dog. Herding breeds and working breeds are typically harder to fix. There are a couple tricks to fixing this.

One that can work almost instantly or your dog won't care at all, is the yelping method. If your dog bites too hard and you give a high-pitched yelp as though you've been hurt, it can stop it instantly. On the other hand, your dog might just assume you're playing and play more rough. This method is not very reliable, but because some dogs care and it takes no time to do so, you might as well give it a try because sometimes it works wonders.

Another option, which is tedious, but the most common method, is replacing your hand for a toy. As soon as they start to bite you, move your hand away and replace it with a toy. I would not use treats during this. You will technically be rewarding the bad behavior. The dog bites your hand, you replace your hand with a toy and then give the dog a treat, it will start to learn when they bite your hand, they get a treat. When doing this method, if it is black and white for the dog, it will be easier for the dog to understand. If you allow play biting sometimes, but not others it can be confusing. The moment your dog starts biting on you, give it a toy. If your dog still tries to bite you, stop play time. Just walk away.

These are all methods which can work, but they can take a long time. When we work with your dog, we will teach "OFF" (which means move away physically and mentally, but not that your dog is not in trouble) which is important because I don't want your dog to think you're mad or playing is bad. Just "hey knock it off". However, the options above can work until we work with your dog.

STORY TIME

My dog Achilles is a Belgian Malinois and his dad did Mondioring in France, so he was bred to bite. Achilles loves to play fight, and communicates through his mouth while nibbling. If you have a dog like Achilles and you try to push them off, run away, or yelp, he will immediately think you're playing and comes at you way harder. With a working breed, they need something to do. You need to replace yourself with a toy. This is harder because you're more fun to play with. You move and make sounds. You get them tug toys, or some type of toy that you can put in their mouth.

HEALTH CARE

There is no medical advice found in this book. Go get this advice from your veterinarian. However, I can give some advice on how to find a veterinarian you can trust. Veterinarians are a lot like dog trainers in the sense when you talk to them, they all will have varying opinions on a lot of things. To sum this section up: keep trying new veterinarians until you find one you can trust. I'll give you an example from personal experience. When I first moved to Nashville, I did not have a veterinarian that I trusted yet. My dog Achilles was having issues itching all the time, and he had this weird spot on his nose that appeared randomly. I went to three different veterinarians to get opinions, and all three gave different answers.

The first one I picked, because it was the closest to where I lived. They told me I needed to change his diet, and they needed to sedate him to do surgery to remove the spot from his nose.

The second one, I picked because I asked a friend of mine at the gym who they used. They said that they needed to put medication on the spot and see if that healed it, and come back in a couple weeks to follow up with it to make sure it wasn't cancer. For the itching, they said I should take him to the dermatologist (which happened to be a parent company for that veterinarian).

The last veterinarian I picked, because it was close and had the most positive Google reviews. This veterinarian said to just leave the nose alone, and it would be gone in a couple of weeks. If it got worse, to come back in. They also said, based on what I told them, it couldn't possibly be the food causing it, so switching food wouldn't work. He needed a shot of Cytopoint.

I used my intuition and used the veterinarian that made the most logical sense to me. When first looking, you want to visit multiple veterinarians and decide for yourself who is best for your furbaby!

LITTERMATES

If you have littermates, this can be a great thing. However, you will want to separate them as much as you can. The reason being is littermates are very prone to having severe separation anxiety. I once had a first 50 cent lesson with two German shepherds who were littermates. We met at a park, and if you pulled them farther than 6 feet from each other, they both would start to thrash on the leash, bark, whine, and sled dog towards each other. The parents said if they tried to walk one of them and leave the other at home, the one left at home would destroy the blinds and scratch at the front door while barking and whining for the whole neighborhood to hear. The dog outside wasn't quite as bad, but it wouldn't even want to go on the walk and It would pull towards the house. We helped them a lot, and now they can leave one at the house and go on walks, and they are both happier and living a better life, however, most of this could've been avoided in the early stages.

Basically the advice here is simplified, if you have littermates, separate them as much as possible for the first year of their life. You will 100% need to kennel train them. Refer to the earlier section in this chapter if you need more information on kennel training. Here is a list of ways to separate them: Have them eat and sleep in separate kennels which are in separate rooms. You might be thinking this is extreme but you must get them used to doing things without seeing or hearing the other one. When you do this over and over it becomes just a way of life.

Every chance you get, take one with you while you leave the other one. If you go on a walk, take one at a time. If you go to a friend's place, take one and leave the other. You do not have to do this every single time, and obviously they are allowed to do stuff together but do it as often as possible. The goal is to teach them that being away from each other is a normal way of life.

The most important part of this is having them eat separately. I'm going to walk you through how and why to do it. The way you do this is to put them in their kennel in separate rooms, put the food in the kennel, and close the kennel. They get 15 minutes to eat. If they don't eat, then the food goes back up, and they don't see it until their next time to eat. You might have to do this 3 or 4 times. The reason you're doing this is because we are teaching the dog to control their emotions and self regulate their anxiety. The first couple times they might not eat, but eventually they will think to themselves "I hate being in this kennel land, I really need to be with my sibling…However, I'm starving." They will take a metaphorical deep breath, start to relax, and begin to eat. Over time, I will teach them that when they feel like this, they need to take that deep breath.

ANXIETY

Anxiety will mostly be handled in the Aggression and Anxiety Chapter, but I want to help you make sure you're not inadvertently training your puppy to have anxiety. Your dog does not understand English (or Spanish) so refer to the chapter - 10 Virtues of dog training for more on this. If you put your dog in a kennel or separate room and they start whining and you go back to them they immediately learn "Oh, when I whine and throw a fit my parents come back to me." You need to ignore the dog when they are whining. The younger you start the dog, the easier it will be. You're creating the picture for the dog (refer to chapter 1). So if you put them in the laundry room, and it starts scratching at the door and whining and barking and you come back in and say "hey buddy you're fine. Dad is right outside", the dog doesn't understand what you're saying. All it understands is it whined and it got dads attention. On the other hand, if you come back in and yell at the dog, it starts to think "Dang every time I go in the kennel, dad yells at me. I really hate being put in here."

When you come home and leave, do not make it a big deal. I would ignore the dog for a couple minutes, and then you can play with them and be excited. If not, you're training the dog to jump on you and go crazy the moment you walk through the door. Which might be cute while they are small, but it won't be when they are grown and you want your grandma to come over, but Fluffy is trained to jump on everyone.

Example: Think about when you leave the house and you say to your dog:

Mom: "Oh my gosh, Fluffy, mom's going to work. Have a great day. I'll miss you! See you when I get home!"

What the dog hears: "Bye, Fluffy, mom is going to work and I might die. Hopefully I make it home if bad things don't happen".

Then after work you come in super excited

Mom: "Oh my gosh, Fluffy, how are you! I missed you so much".

What the dog hears: "Oh no, Fluffy. I can't believe I made it home! I almost died, there are so many monsters out there. Please freak out because this is a big deal".

Even if the dog magically understands English, you're still conditioning the dog to go crazy every time you leave and come home. Your dog starts to think that's what's expected.

Want to open your own Make Your Dog Epic dog training business?
Learn how to have your own! Open one of the most affordable and turn-key dog training businesses on the planet at MakeYourDogEpic.com.

PUPPY HABITS, GROWN-UP TRAITS

You must understand that the behaviors that are cute and adorable while they are little will most likely not be adorable when they are big. For example, jumping and whining to get in your lap. Think about a 3 month old Husky puppy.

This is possibly one of the cutest puppies. When they are jumping on you and whining, it's very cute and adorable and it melts your heart. So you give them attention each time they do it. However, that cute little puppy that was about 10-20 pounds turns into this.

Which is still cute and adorable, but now you've taught it that if it jumps, it gets attention. So now when grandma comes over, you have a dog that jumps on her for attention.

STORY TIME

When I got Achilles, I gave him a couple weeks without training because I wanted to take that time to bond with him and give him a chance to adjust before immediately training him. I took him to see my family because they wanted to meet him. He immediately ran over to my grandma and jumped on her. I had to catch her before she hit the ground. She said "Some dog trainer you are," she was not very pleased hah! Even though he was a cute little dog at that weight and size, having a baby Belgian Malinois is like owning a baby velociraptor. I want to show you three progressions, which are all photos before he was a year and a half old.

He went from this:

To this:

Want to open your own Make Your Dog Epic dog training business?
Learn how to have your own! Open one of the most affordable and turn-key dog training businesses on the planet at MakeYourDogEpic.com.

To this:

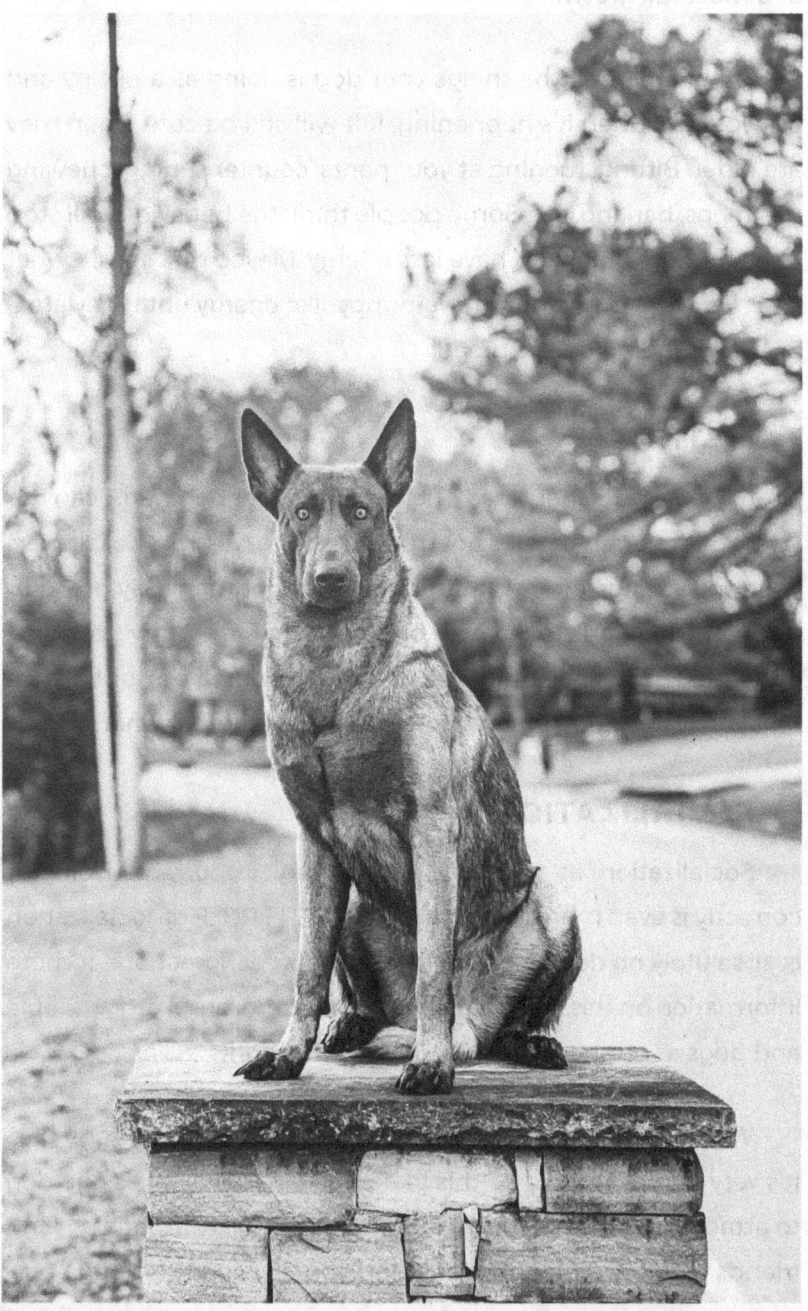

Want to open your own Make Your Dog Epic dog training business? Learn how to have your own! Open one of the most affordable and turn-key dog training businesses on the planet at MakeYourDogEpic.com.

Now at any of these sizes, jumping is an issue, but especially at almost full grown.

Think about all the things your dog is doing as a puppy and ask yourself when it's happening, if it will still be cute when they are older. Bitting, tugging at your pants, counter surfing, chewing up things, barking, etc. Some people think the behaviors will stop once they are older and have less energy. Maybe that's somewhat true. However, some dogs have puppy-like energy until they are 9 or 10 depending on the breed.

MYTH

If I get my dog neutered, they will be better behaved. I can not stress this enough that it's not true in any way. Yes, maybe it lowers your dog's testosterone a little bit. But it's not magically going to get your dog to listen better or stop being aggressive towards other dogs. Never neuter your dog if it is purely for obedience reasons. Never neuter a man for obedience reasons either.

SOCIALIZATION

Socialization at an early age is very important. Doing it correctly is even more important. NUMBER 1 RULE of socialization is absolutely no dog parks. Refer to the dog park section for more information on this. You want to get your dog around other people and dogs as often as possible. Just no dog parks.

We will start with getting your dog around other dogs first. It's very important you do this in a safe way. It only takes one dog to attack your dog for your dog to have that 'picture' forever. Find friends who have friendly dogs, and you all can have doggy play dates with them. You can also set it up to where you pass them on walks, and let your dog say hi to them. This way, they get used to other dogs being friendly.

With humans, a trick is when you have people over or when you are out in public, you can give the other people treats. Then when your dog walks up to them and says "hi", have them give your dog a treat. If you have a more timid dog, this might take longer. If you have an already outgoing dog, the people might not even need treats and just petting the dog will be plenty of excitement.

I will address something that I am sure someone out there is arguing with me on. "When training you want your dog focused on you. If you do these steps the dog will be more focused on other dogs and people than you and you will have a hard time getting the dog to focus on you." My rebuttal to this would be "That's true. However, it is always easier to train a dog to focus on

PAWS, for a Fun Fact

Your dog can smell 40x better than you can.
- MontecitoPetHospital.com

you than it is to train a dog who doesn't like people or dogs, to like people or dogs. Every single time". Do not worry about this. Obedience is always fixable. Anxiety and aggression is not. When in doubt, I would always rather have your dog like humans and dogs "too much"

DESENSITIZATION

Desensitization early is important. You want to think of all the typical things you know of dogs not liking and do that with your puppy. Sounds strange, but the more you do it, the more it's a normal thing and not some massive event. For example: Car rides, tail, ear, paws, nails, getting in the tub, being in the kennel, being held, walking with other people, staying with other people. Anything you can think of that you've seen dogs not like. You want to take your dog with you as often as you can in the car that way they are used to it. I'll use my dog Achilles as an example. While he was a puppy, I would take him on car rides all the time. While we were driving, I would mess with his ears, feel his paws, as well as hold them. I would also randomly hold his tail. I know he is a Belgian Malinois and was bred to do MondioRing. That's what his dad and mom did. So he has all those genetic traits however, I needed him around kids and people. I was very intentional about doing things like randomly putting him in the bathtub and kennel training him so he was used to it. The more you do each thing the more normal it becomes. Now kids lay on top of him and smother him and he is completely fine!

PAWS, for a Notable Quotable

"Drifting, without aim or purpose, is the first cause of failure."

-NAPOLEON HILL
(The best-selling author of Think & Grow Rich.)

Want to open your own Make Your Dog Epic dog training business?
Learn how to have your own! Open one of the most affordable and turn-key dog training businesses on the planet at MakeYourDogEpic.com.

PAWS, for a Notable Quotable

"He that walketh with wise men shall be wise: But a companion of fools shall be destroyed."

- PROVERBS 13:20

(King James Version)

Want to open your own Make Your Dog Epic dog training business?
Learn how to have your own! Open one of the most affordable and turn-key dog training businesses on the planet at MakeYourDogEpic.com.

CHAPTER 5
Potty Training

JOKE TIME
Q: Which dog breed is guaranteed to laugh at all of your jokes?
A: A Chi-ha-ha!

THE GUIDE TO PUPPY POTTY TRAINING: 9 STEPS TO SUCCESS

Unless you hate your life and want your home to smell like dog excrement, potty training your puppy is a crucial step in raising a well-behaved and happy puppy. Establishing a routine, using positive reinforcement, and understanding your puppy's cues are the keys to success. In this guide, we will walk you through a 9 step process to make potty training easier and more effective, along with some do's and don'ts to ensure a smooth journey. Remember, patience and consistency are key! Good luck! We understand potty training is one, if not the most frustrating part of dog training. Our goal is to simplify the process for you. The process is tedious, and possibly annoying, but WAY less annoying than picking up pee and poop everyday!

PAWS,
for a Fun Fact

Watch your step! It only takes one step to know if your dog needs more potty training.

Want to open your own Make Your Dog Epic dog training business?
Learn how to have your own! Open one of the most affordable and turn-key dog training businesses on the planet at MakeYourDogEpic.com.

9 Steps to Potty Training:

STEP #1- BEGIN YOUR DAY EARLY

Start your day by taking your puppy outside in the morning. On average, puppies can hold their bladder one hour per month of age, so this morning trip sets the tone for the day and helps establish a routine. This is dependent on the dog's age, breed, and size. There is no one size fits all for the amount of time for puppies.

STEP #2- LET THEM CHOOSE THEIR SPOT

Allow your puppy to choose their potty spot during this morning outing. Have them on leash to keep them from distractions. They can lead you but if they start eating stuff or playing with stuff keep them moving. They will mark this spot, and it will become their designated potty area during training. However, keep them on a leash to ensure they cannot get too distracted. Each puppy is unique, so let them explore and pick their preferred potty spot. Once they find their spot you should continue taking them to that spot every single time.

STEP #3- NOW DON'T LET THEM CHOOSE THEIR SPOT

After those first couple take outs with your new puppy, now you need to start taking them to the same area every time. Have them on a leash so they can not get super distracted. When they get into a habit of going to the same spot over and over, it will start to become easier, and easier. They should only get a maximum of 10-15 minutes to go potty.

Want to open your own Make Your Dog Epic dog training business?
Learn how to have your own! Open one of the most affordable and turn-key dog training businesses on the planet at MakeYourDogEpic.com.

STEP #4- POSITIVE REINFORCEMENT

Keep repeating "go potty" until they do. Praise your puppy enthusiastically every time they use the designated potty spot. You can also offer a treat to reinforce the behavior and make it more enjoyable. Be Careful with this step and make sure you are rewarding the correct behavior. Do not reward them when they get back inside. Reward them right away. Caveat to this rule: if your dog loves treats so much they won't go potty because they are so focused on you, then do not use treats.

STEP #5- IF THEY DON'T GO POTTY

This is the most tedious part and will test your patience a lot. It is also the most vital. If your puppy does not go potty, you need to bring the puppy back in and immediately have it go in its kennel. The kennel should not be a bad thing at this point because you have made it a fun place. Refer to the puppy chapter of this book for more information on kennels.

STEP #6- KENNEL SOILING

If your kennel is too spacious and the dog can pee and poop on one side and sleep on the other side then the kennel is too big. Consider getting a smaller kennel or using partitions to limit space. Yes, this means a couple times you will need to clean pee off your dog.

STEP #7- KENNEL SOILING: THE BAD NEWS

If your dog's kennel is small enough and it's peeing all over itself, that means it genuinely can not hold it and you need to let the puppy out more often. If you're letting your dog out frequently and it continues doing this after weeks of training, unfortunately you may have one of the very rare cases of a dog that simply does not care about it. Talk to a trainer if this is the case.

STEP #8- NEVER EVER

Never rub your dog's nose in the mess. They do not know! They only know that you came home and are pissed. The dogs timing is VERY important! If it does not happen immediately after the dog will not associate them going potty in the house with the punishment. Even if you manage to time it perfectly and the dog understands, it's not a good way to punish them because this will just create sneaky dogs. You will just teach the dog to do it where you won't see them. Which means now they will do it in the other room, the closet, and even under the bed.

STEP #9- CREATE A SCHEDULE

The more strict you are on a schedule, the quicker the potty training will happen. Do not free feed or it will be IMPOSSIBLE to create a schedule with your dog. Feed them at designated times, and only let them get 20 minutes to eat. If they don't eat, the food goes up until the next designated feeding time. If the dog is used to free feeding, it might not eat the first couple times. Your dog will start to understand. The key thing to watch is how soon the dog is using the bathroom after and create the potty schedule accordingly.

FREQUENTLY ASKED POTTY TRAINING QUESTIONS

1. How Do I Recognize When My Puppy Needs to Go?

Watch for signs like whining, barking, restlessness, pacing, sniffing, or circling. These cues indicate your puppy needs a potty break. You should also create a schedule with the dog. You should know how long it takes for them to digest their food.

2. How Long Does Potty Training Take?

Potty training duration varies depending on age, breed, and the individual dog itself. It can take a few weeks to up to six months for complete potty training.

3. How Should I Handle Mistakes?

React calmly and never punish your puppy for accidents. Interrupt them with a loud clap or a noise, but not an angry yell if you catch them in the act, and take them to the designated potty spot. If your dog knows the "OFF" command, you may use that as well. Clean accidents thoroughly to remove odors. Using punishment will only teach them to be more sneaky and do it when you're not watching or in the closet. Never leave copious amounts of urine and dog feces around your home, never live with twelve dogs, and don't become a hoarder. Also, choose now to never become weak, feeble, frail, soft, wimpish, slight, tender, lame, wimpy, passive aggressive, and a double-minded, back-stabbing, greedy person.

4. Can I Use Potty Pads?

While potty pads can be convenient in some situations, using them can confuse your dog. It's best to prioritize outdoor potty training to avoid mixed signals. A potty pad feels a lot like carpet or a rug so it can be confusing. If you are in an apartment complex with a balcony, you may use them there. However, never use them inside. Unless you have a small breed that will never be potty trained because their bladder is genuinely too small.

5. Shouldn't We Be Getting Results Faster?

It's essential to understand potty training takes time and patience. Some dog owners expect instant results, but every dog is unique, and the learning process varies. Don't be discouraged by occasional setbacks; consistency is the key to success.

MYTH CORRECTION

> "My dog knows he did something bad because when I come home and see the mess and look at him his ears are back or he goes and hides in his Kennel."

WRONG!

Your dog understands your blood pressure is rising and you're upset. You have conditioned your dog to be scared and run to its kennel when it senses this.

Conclusion:

Potty training is a journey that demands patience, consistency, and the right approach. By following these tips and dispelling common myths, you can successfully potty train your dog. Remember that each dog is unique, so adapt your training to their specific needs. If you require further guidance, reach out to our team and we will help guide you through the process. Potty training can be a rewarding experience, strengthening the bond between you and your four-legged companion.

PAWS, for a Fun Fact

Dogs sniff rear ends as their way of asking "who are you and how have you been?".

- MentalFloss.com

Want to open your own Make Your Dog Epic dog training business? Learn how to have your own! Open one of the most affordable and turn-key dog training businesses on the planet at MakeYourDogEpic.com.

PAWS, for a Notable Quotable

"All successful people men and women are big dreamers. They imagine what their future could be, ideal in every respect, and then they work every day toward their distant vision, that goal or purpose."

- **BRIAN TRACY**

(Best-selling author, world-class trainer, motivational speaker and sales trainer.)

Want to open your own Make Your Dog Epic dog training business?
Learn how to have your own! Open one of the most affordable and turn-key dog training businesses on the planet at MakeYourDogEpic.com.

CHAPTER 6
10 Sins Of Dog Training

JOKE TIME
Q: Where do dogs hate to shop?
A: The flea market!

#1 - LEASHES THAT EXTEND

I understand the appeal of leashes that extend. Before I started my dog training journey, I used extendable leashes all the time. You can give your dog more freedom to potty or play when you want, or you can keep the dog close if you need to. Which sounds GREAT! However, think about what the dog is seeing. Your dog thinks "sometimes when I pull I get to go farther away and I get to go where I want. I'll just start pulling all the time!" Now you have accidentally taught your dog to pull on the leash.

#2 - HARNESSES

Disclaimer: I understand that some dogs need to be on a harness for a reason that your veterinarian said. If that is the case ignore this.

For the majority of people, they typically switch to a harness because the dog is pulling so hard its choking itself or they feel like it gives them more control. Or they use the front of the Harness because it mitigates the pulling a little bit. Think about any sled dog ever. They all wear harnesses because they can pull with absolutely no restraint.

Want to open your own Make Your Dog Epic dog training business? Learn how to have your own! Open one of the most affordable and turn-key dog training businesses on the planet at MakeYourDogEpic.com.

They have the collar attached but it's for "direction" to keep them in the straight line.

You have good intentions, but you're creating a sled dog. Dog trainers use harnesses to make dogs want to pull harder towards things. They use harnesses so the dog can pull, but there is no negative restraint.

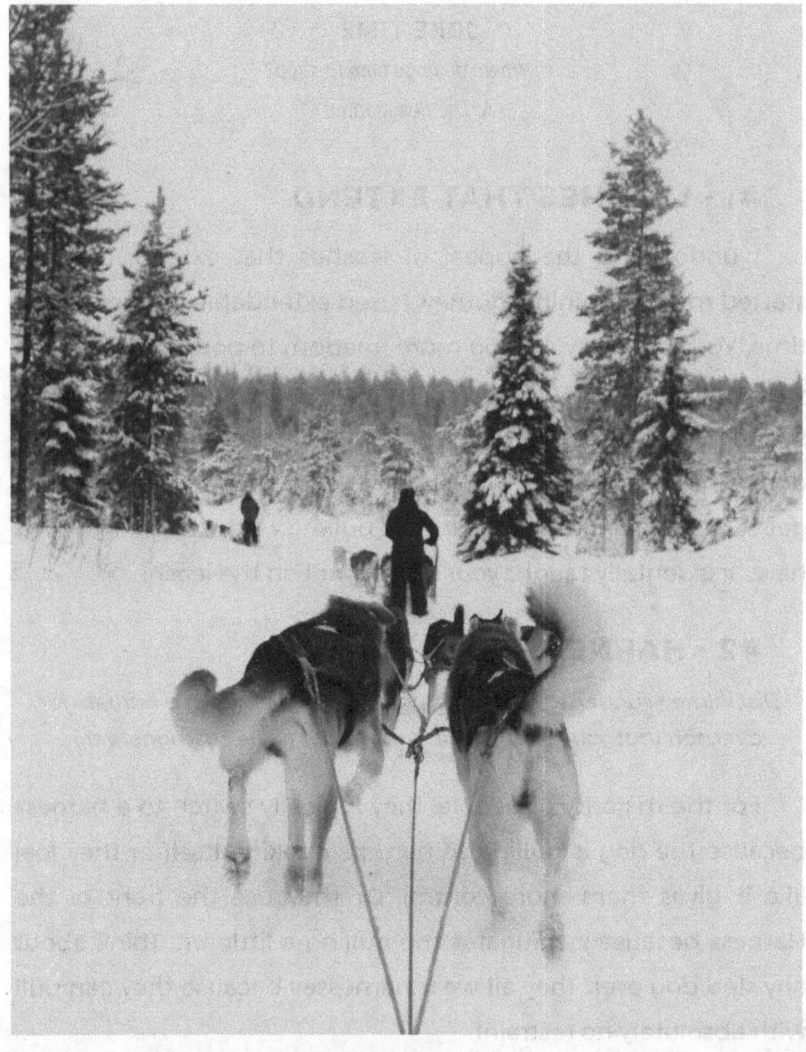

Want to open your own Make Your Dog Epic dog training business? Learn how to have your own! Open one of the most affordable and turn-key dog training businesses on the planet at MakeYourDogEpic.com.

#3 - DOG PARKS

Dog parks are the one thing I would say most dog trainers are on the same page about. They are an absolute NO! I'm going to give you real life examples of things I have heard in our 50 cent lessons.

I did a 50 cent first lesson with a 3 year old Schnauzer. These are their actual words.

> **Them**: "We want to work on obedience and I guess socialization. We think socialization is under control. We are taking him to the dog park. It's gone pretty well. He has been in a couple dog fights, but we know its just about repetition and practice. But we are struggling a lot with his obedience"
>
> **Me**: "You say a couple fights. How many is that? Tell me about it."
>
> **Them**: "Well It's like 7-8 ish fights. Its for sure less than 15. But he hasn't gotten into a fight in like half a year."
>
> **Me**: "When was the last time you went to the dog park?"
>
> **Them**: "About sixish months ago."

This is a real conversation of many that I wish I was making up. But their dog has gotten into many dog fights at the dog park and they think the solution is to keep going to the dog park.

Want to open your own Make Your Dog Epic dog training business?
Learn how to have your own! Open one of the most affordable and turn-key dog training businesses on the planet at MakeYourDogEpic.com.

Now, you might be thinking "Well sure that person needs to stop going to the dog park obviously but my dog isn't aggressive so it's fine". This issue with this is it just takes one dog to attack your dog for your dog to be aggressive or skittish forever. Dogs don't think rationally like humans do, they see in pictures. If you walk into a store and someone randomly punches you in the face as a human you can think "ok well that sucks but it's not what's going to happen every time." With dogs you have fight or flight and they don't think rationally. So depending on the dog, sometimes it just takes once. If the dog is confident it will think "I'm going to attack these dogs before they can attack me" with a non confident dog they think "at any moment one of these dogs could attack me"

Instead of just talking about how bad dog parks are, I'm going to give you solutions to the 3 main reasons people go to dog parks. I understand you want to get your dog socialization, exercise, and give the dog off leash freedom.

Off leash freedom: You fix that with one of two solutions. Option one is to train the dog so their "COME" command is proofed. That's how you get full off leash freedom. Option two is find someone else that has a yard big enough you can go where your dog can run around.

Exercise: This one has unlimited solutions. Dog Treadmill, walks, fetch, hire a dog walker, hire a squirrel trainer to have it run in a circle around the yard while your dog chases it. (Just kidding PETA)

Socialization: When in doubt, talk to a reputable trainer about this one. This one is very different on a case by case basis.

You can get a group of people together who have dogs that all get along. They can all play together. Just make sure any dogs that have not met before, are introduced slowly to each dog. Don't just throw them into the group, it can be very overwhelming. This is a great solution if you love all the things about the dog park. Have a group of people with dogs you trust, and let them all play together. The main issue with dog parks is too many dogs at a time and people bring aggressive dogs all the time. You don't want their negligence to affect your dog's life.

#4 - STARTING WITH HIGH VALUE THINGS

This one isn't a major deal, it's just a pro tip with treat training. Think of treats and toys from now on as high and low value. For example a dog that doesn't like toys. The toy no matter what toy is low value because he doesn't care about it. I'll use my dog Achilles for example because he is a good mix. My other dog Riley is psycho for all toys and treats. For her the best toy is a tennis ball but it is only slightly above everything else.

WITH ACHILLES IT GOES LIKE THIS:

- **Other animals like goats, chickens, squirrels.**
- **Steak or chicken**
- **His dog food**

- **Playing with dogs**
- **Playing rough with dad**
- **Kids**
- **The green squishy fetch ball**
- **Other people**
- **Water buffalo horn**
- **Other toys**

Scarcity breeds value in dogs. What do I mean by this? If I leave frisbees out all the time where the dog has access to it, they start to lose their value. However, if I only bring the frisbee out for short spurts like when the dog is training, then they start to crave the frisbee even more.

I'll explain this in human terms. When I went through basic training for the Army, I went 4 months without seeing my phone. For two months I never heard music. Then we took a bus to a training exercise and the driver played music. I realized in the moment how much I valued and took music for granted. The music on the bus had my complete attention. I started listening very closely to the lyrics, and how the beat and chords in the music made me feel. This was a massive endorphin release. Before basic training music would just be in the background and wasn't a big deal. Kind-of like when you were a kid, coloring books were AWESOME! Until you discovered video games and smartphones. It's the same for dogs if the thing is always around it loses value. A big mistake that people make in treat training is they start with super high value things like steak but now you're stuck using that every time because it means more than any other treat. However, overall it means less because it's readily available. But because the squirrel is not always there, it already meant more to the dog than steak did. Now when the dog sees the squirrel it could care less about the steak, it just wants the squirrel.

#5 - LABELING BEFORE IT'S CLEAR

Think about how many times you said "sit" the first time you tried to get your dog to sit. Most people say it like 4 times before the dog sits. That's because they inadvertently taught the dog that the command is "sit sit sit sit". The dog thinks on the 4th command if ever then it has to sit. Or it thinks it can sit whenever it feels like it. One thing that we do differently at Make Your Dog Epic is we don't label commands until they are clear. We teach the dog the action first and have them do it until they understand what we want from them. Then we label it. (Label means to overlay a word with an action) The reason we do this is because our goal in training is: Clarity for the dog, least amount of bad reps as possible, and the dog listens for the first time everytime to commands.

#6 - ASKING AND NOT TELLING

This goes along with the last section. I am absolutely positive you have done this or heard someone else do it. They say in a super soft voice "can you sit?" and it sounds like a question. Or they ask in a baby voice. You should never raise your voice (unless your dog is far away obviously). However, the commands should be you telling the dog what to do not asking. There are several reasons for this behavior. Firstly, if you're constantly asking the dogs, they're likely to ignore you. However, the primary reason is that if you always ask in a gentle tone but suddenly switch to a stern voice, particularly by the fourth command, your dog might start feeling as though it's in trouble. This can lead to a loss of its personality or a fear of training altogether, as the dog associates training with the expectation of being scolded by its owner.

#7 - OVER USING "GOOD"

If you use good to "release the dog" and use good to tell them they are doing good, it's confusing and you dilute the meaning of the word "good". Remember dogs see in pictures. Most people have a hard time getting their dog to "stay". One of the reasons is because of how they use "good". I'll explain how most people teach 'SIT' and by this point in the book you should be able to point out why it's confusing for the dog.

First the person stands over the dog and says "sit, sit, sit" finally the dog sits and the trainer says "GOOOD" then the dog gets up and gets a treat. Next step is they keep going until the dog gets better and now when it sits the trainer says " good..... gooooood" then gives the release word. However, they can't get the dog to stay for more than 15 seconds. This is because the same word they are using to "release" the dog is the same word they are using to tell the dog it is doing good. They now also use the word good for everything. Now over time the word gets diluted, and means less and less also, it means more and more at the same time.

TO THE DOG "GOOD" MEANS:

- **Be excited**
- **That's correct**
- **Release**
- **Keep sitting**

If you're confused at this point at least you and the dog have something in common. When training dogs, use as few words as possible and make sure you're saying them in a consistent manner. You want to make it as clear as possible for the dog.

#8 - STAAAYYYYYY

You should not be saying "Staaayyyyyy" to your dog. It's the equivalent of saying "readyyy seeeeeeet GO!" You are amping the dog up, not actually helping. You should also just keep repeating the command that they are doing. If they are sitting, give a reminder with the command "sit" if they are in a 'DOWN' say "down" to keep them in a down. Remember it's not "doowwwwwnnn" it's just "down"

#9 - GIVING ATTENTION WHILE IN THE KENNEL

This is one that might be the most frustrating and hardest. It is where most people fail in kennel training. The dog pulls at the heart strings of the owner. The dog whines and the owner feels bad. So they go up to the dog's kennel and say things like "you're ok, buddy." Or they yell at the dog to shut up. Let's look at it from the dog's perspective.

Mom puts me in a kennel - she leaves and I don't want to be in here - I whine and bark - mom walks back in and makes noises that I don't understand (dogs don't speak english incase you forgot) - She leaves - well I didn't get out of the kennel but at least I got attention. - mom walks in again - I start barking and whining - mom lets me out - ohh it must be because I whined and barked. Nice! That's all I have to do and I get out.

By doing this you're making the problem worse. Now obviously If you train with us we will teach the dog "QUIET" and fix it quickly but you can make it easier on yourself by not giving in when you first start. Just ignore the dog while they are barking or whining.

10 - NOT HAVING A GAME PLAN AND A GOAL

Everytime you start a training session you should have a goal of where you want to get to. You also should have a game plan of how to get there. I see it too often, where trainers start training a dog and they literally let the dog lead the session. They train reactively instead of proactively. This is about 20% of trainers.

I would say the next level up is trainers who have a goal but not necessarily a game plan to get there. They purely train on how the dog is doing. Which sounds good but there are a couple massive issues with this. First issue, is your system should work on all dogs so you should have a system and game plan. The second, is you train just reactively which is a huge no go. You should be leading the session.

Want to open your own Make Your Dog Epic dog training business?
Learn how to have your own! Open one of the most affordable and turn-key dog training businesses on the planet at MakeYourDogEpic.com.

The next is the more diligent trainer. They have a goal and a game plan to get to that goal. However, an issue most have is because they are diligent they get off track worrying about little perfections. They forget the main purpose of the training session because they see the dog not doing a different command perfectly. I'll give an example. A trainer is working "PLACE", they are "HEELING" the dog over to the place spot so they can work it. However the dog keeps messing up on "HEEL" so they stop the whole session to work "HEEL", but the goal of the session was to work "PLACE". Now they have changed a "PLACE" session into a "HEELING" session. If you can fix the issue quick then great! But if it's going to change the course of the session then don't do it. **In short, train proactively not reactively!**

PAWS,
for a Fun Fact

Dogs dog to beat the heat. When stuck on an open lawn with little or no shade, unearthing a fresh layer of dirt untouched by sun is a quick way to cool down.

- *MentalFloss.com*

PAWS, for a Notable Quotable

"In a crowded marketplace, fitting in is failing. In a busy marketplace, not standing out is the same as being invisible."

- SETH GODIN

(Seth Godin is an author, entrepreneur and most of all, a teacher. Seth is an entrepreneur, best-selling author, and speaker.)

Want to open your own Make Your Dog Epic dog training business? Learn how to have your own! Open one of the most affordable and turn-key dog training businesses on the planet at MakeYourDogEpic.com.

CHAPTER 7

10 Virtues Of Dog Training

JOKE TIME

Q: What did one flea say to the other?
A: Should we walk or take the dog?

#1 - UNDERSTANDING YOUR DOG DOES NOT UNDERSTAND ENGLISH

This is one we see a lot! If you want to communicate well with your dog and be a good dog trainer or owner, you need to understand your dog does not understand what you're saying. Examples:

- "Fluffy can you sit?"
- "It's ok buddy, that dog isn't going to hurt you."
- "Fluffy get over here and stop doing that!"
- "Be gentle, easy, wait, stayyyyy!"

As an example: Your dog has no idea what you're saying. Let's use going past another dog on a walk. Your dog typically growls and barks at other dogs when they walk by. You're on a walk and you see a dog in the distance, so you start saying in a sweet voice "hey buddy you're fine it's ok" now you crouch down next to him and start petting him. He has absolutely no idea what you're saying. However, he does know that all the other times he has barked at other dogs you start making those noises. He also knows that you are anxious and can sense your blood pressure rising. Which he knows every time that has happened before, he has been trying to attack another dog. So now instead of calming the dog down like you believe you are, it's like putting gasoline on a fire.

Instead of doing this you need to teach your dog what commands actually mean and teach them to do that. So in this example you would teach 'COME' or 'OFF'. Let's use 'COME' as an example: You would wait until your dog starts pulling or right before it does pull you would say "COME" and bring the dog back to you. You do that over and over so you're changing the dog's picture of the situation. So instead of mom saying sentences the dog doesn't understand and her blood pressure rising, the dog learns "oh when I feel like this mom is going to tell me to come and I'll have to go back to her."

#2 - UNDERSTANDING THE 4 VARIABLES

Rule: Only change 1 variable at a time.

While you are training dogs there are 4 variables you can change. Distance, body language, distraction, and the leash. Remember dogs see in pictures, if you change a variable it could be like changing the whole picture for the dog. So I'll give an example of each while working 'COME':

Distance - If you're working 'COME' from 5 feet away, changing to 10 feet away is changing the distance variable.

Want to open your own Make Your Dog Epic dog training business? Learn how to have your own! Open one of the most affordable and turn-key dog training businesses on the planet at MakeYourDogEpic.com.

Body Language - when starting 'COME' you want to squat down. Universally, for dogs this is a more inviting position. This is normally the position people are in when they pet them and love them. How you change this picture is by not squatting all the way down or standing up, which changes the body language variable.

Distraction - As almost everyone understands when they try to train their own dog for the first time, it listens inside but not outside. Anything that gets the dog's attention off you is changing the variable of distraction.

Leash - At the beginning of teaching 'COME', you want to give leash direction towards you with the leash. Not pull, but just tension. As you stop giving tension on the leash, that is changing the leash variable.

#3 - TAKING A STEP BACK TO GO FORWARD

Read the previous section on the three variables before reading this.

The better you get at dog training, the fewer bad reps you should be getting. However, it is inevitable when you are learning or if you are a client, you will get some bad reps. While training, you should think of each training session as a scoreboard on the left side there is 'good reps', on the right side there is 'bad reps'. Each time the dog does something good, the good reps get a point. Each time the dog does something bad, the bad side gets a point. At minimum for each bad rep, you should get 3 good reps. So in each training session it should be 75% good, 25% bad, which is a worse-case scenario. Keep track of that score board in your mind.

What is a good rep? A good rep is if the dog is getting better. No matter what command you're working, the dog is progressing in training. If the answer is not yes then it is a bad rep.

Let's say you are working 'COME' and all of the sudden you start getting multiple bad reps. Good news, and good news. Good news It's your fault as the trainer, not the dog's fault. Good news is that because it's your fault you can fix it. When you start getting bad reps it is typically because you changed more than one variable while training whether you realized it or not. The other option is you are not being as precise with your body language or leash as you should be. Either way, if you start getting bad reps you need to take a step back to make it easier on the dog. You take a step back by reinserting one of the variables you took away or changed.

For example: if you start getting bad reps while working, 'COME'. You just changed from crouching to standing and you tell the dog to "COME" and it seems like the dog has no idea what you were asking it to do. If you get multiple bad reps and you feel the training session is deteriorating, you need to add back in crouching so you can start getting good reps again. Then as they are doing better phase the variable back out.

If you're a newer trainer and you tell me this happened I automatically assume you either moved on too fast and the dog wasn't ready or you changed two variables at once.

As you start getting better you should have to do this less and less. This rule should not exist when you are a GREAT trainer.

#4 - FAST DOGS GO SLOW, SLOW DOGS GO FAST

Pace with dogs matters a lot. With a dog that does everything super fast while training you need to slow everything down and make it very clear for them. If you try to speed through training with a fast dog they will get more and more frantic. Fast dogs once trained are awesome! However, for most people they are typically the most frustrating to train. That's because for them their brain moves as fast as their body. It is like a kid with ADHD, you must slow everything down and make it clear. If you do this correctly, it will make your training much easier. With fast dogs, you will always be able to speed them back up, but in the mean time slow everything down.

Slow dogs you can go faster with and you should. What I mean by this, is you should constantly be trying to speed the dog up and keep the training fun and exciting. When I say go fast I don't mean in your progression of training, I mean by speeding up how fast you walk and talk. *When in doubt, the fastest way to train a dog is slow.*

#5 - USING THE LEASH AS A JOYSTICK

When you are training any dog, view the leash as a joystick. Straight up is neutral. From there it is just like a joystick. Forward, left, right, back. The direction you point the leash is the direction you're giving to the dog. This seems obvious but most people aren't conscious of where they are pointing the leash. They will have the dog on their left side, have the leash pointed backwards and with the right hand point for the dog to move forward to a 'PLACE' spot. You can not have off leash training without first having great on leash direction.

Want to open your own Make Your Dog Epic dog training business?
Learn how to have your own! Open one of the most affordable and turn-key dog training businesses on the planet at MakeYourDogEpic.com.

#6 - END EVERY TRAINING SESSION ON A GOOD NOTE

When you end a training session it needs to be on a good "picture". Whatever picture you end on is the picture your dog will start the next training session with. Understand, if you're starting to feel frustrated with the training, your dog probably is as well. If you start getting frustrated, go back a step, make it clear and get a couple good reps. Then give the dog massive praise and give them a bunch of pets and end the training session. This will keep the dogs morale and yours very high. If you keep putting the dog up while it's frustrated it will start to associate training time with being frustrated. Which now you've turned what should be a really fun activity for the dog into a really stressful activity for the dog.

#7 - NOT TEACHING 'SHAKE', 'SPEAK', OR 'SPIN'

This main reason for this is because these commands are hard to stop from happening once the dog understands them. They are super cute when you first teach them, or when it's convenient. However, once they start doing it nonstop or when it's inconvenient it's not. All three of these commands I never teach my own dogs. I'll give you my reason and you can decide for yourself if you want to teach it or not.

Shake - I do a lot of events with my dogs. Like home shows, boat shows, baseball games, football games, hockeys games, etc. At those events my dogs are typically on 'PLACE' spots that are high up. Any dog that knows 'SHAKE' does 'SHAKE' for attention because after they do it they typically get a treat or pets. Because of this I don't want them to 'SHAKE' an older person and cut them with their nails or 'SHAKE' and hit a child in the face.

Want to open your own Make Your Dog Epic dog training business? Learn how to have your own! Open one of the most affordable and turn-key dog training businesses on the planet at MakeYourDogEpic.com.

Speak - This one is self explanatory on why you wouldn't want to teach this if you can't shut it off. Typically, trainers teach 'SPEAK' by getting the dog frustrated that they can't have a toy or treat by holding them away from it. Once the dog barks out of frustration, they let the dog go. Then they do it over and over while saying 'SPEAK'. The issue is, now when the dog gets frustrated it thinks to get its way it should bark. Which is what the dog should do because that's what the trainer or owner taught it to do. So when you are giving the dog attention, bark. When you get the toy out and don't give it to them immediately, bark. When it wants to go outside, bark. When you're in public at dinner on a peaceful patio and it wants to get the squirrel but you're holding it back...., Guess what? BARK, BARK, BARK.

Spin - This one is admittedly more of a personal one for me. It is just very frustrating when a dog is taught to spin and when it gets the least bit confused it reverts to spinning. Also, when you 'HEEL' the dog and you turn right, but it spins left to go right. Granted the 'HEEL' is fixable but frustrating at first.

#8 - BEING STRICT WHERE IT MATTERS

When you're training, keep the constant question in your mind "does this matter at this moment?" If you are training the dog to do something new, you want to be aware of what matters and what doesn't. If you're training a dog and they aren't perfect on a past command while you're working the new command does it matter if you fix it? I can't tell you without seeing it. You have to be aware of it yourself. Great trainers understand this well.

Want to open your own Make Your Dog Epic dog training business?
Learn how to have your own! Open one of the most affordable and turn-key dog training businesses on the planet at MakeYourDogEpic.com.

General rule: Remember the goal of the session. If you are going to fix something and it's going to be at the expense of the session, Don't do it.

#9 - WHAT TO LOOK FOR WHEN FINDING A TRAINER

These are my 5 things to look for when looking for a dog trainer.

- **Customer testimonials**
- **Results Oriented**
- **Their dog**
- **See them work with your dog**
- **Guarantee on training**

There are many dog trainers to choose from, and finding the right one for you can be challenging. In the world of dog training, there are no regulations and every trainer certifies themselves. Currently all of my trainers are Make Your Dog Epic Certified. Which, guess what? It means absolutely nothing. The reason being is because there is no governing body over it. There is no one holding us or any dog trainer to a certain standard. When you're looking for dog trainers there are 5 main things I would recommend looking for. I understand while you read this, you're thinking, "He is just saying that because they do all of these things". We are not in every city so we can not reach everyone. My hope is this will help the people we can't personally help find a great trainer near them.

Want to open your own Make Your Dog Epic dog training business? Learn how to have your own! Open one of the most affordable and turn-key dog training businesses on the planet at MakeYourDogEpic.com.

Customer Testimonials - This is possibly the most important. You must read and hear what other people are saying about the training. In the world of dog training, every single dog trainer certifies themselves and claims to be the best. Because of this, you MUST read reviews from past customers. Read with discernment on reviews. Every single business gets bad reviews. You can not please everyone. If you see bad reviews, ask yourself if you would've been mad about that as well. Also, see how the business responded. Did they try to fix the issue or blame the customer? Whatever they did to them there is a high possibility they will do to you.

Results Oriented - In the dog training world so many trainers and customers are focused on the number of lessons. This should not be the focus, the focus should be results! If your dog does 100 lessons but still doesn't listen, what's the point? If the dog does 2 lessons, and does everything you want the dog to be able to do that's more important. You do not want someone selling you an amount of time, you want results.

Their Dog - You want to see the trainer's dog. This is very important. Think about it, if their dog won't listen will they be able to get yours to listen? Typically, when you see a trainer's dog you are seeing the best they can possibly do. If possible, you also want to see the dog in a public place not just where they train. If they only show you their dog at a training facility it's probably because they don't listen around distractions. If they show off their dog to you and you're impressed, and would be thrilled if your dog did that then it's a great sign. A trainer's dog is kind-of like their resume or diploma of sorts. Showing they know what they are talking about.

Want to open your own Make Your Dog Epic dog training business?
Learn how to have your own! Open one of the most affordable and turn-key dog training businesses on the planet at MakeYourDogEpic.com.

See Them Work with Your Dog - This is possibly the most important. You need to see that they don't just speak a good game, they can actually show you. The trainer needs to be able to show you some demonstration of their training skills before you sign up. Seeing their dog is fine. But more importantly you need to see them train your specific dog. Make sure that their training methods are right for you.

Guarantee on Training - Do they offer a money back guarantee on training? If not, what guarantee of training? Too many trainers operate under the "you get what you get and don't throw a fit" method. The other option is the "it might stick" method. Basically, what that means is the training might "stick" so there is a chance after the training is over that the training doesn't work. Ask about guarantees on training, and you want to see if they are dodging the question or not.

Hopefully this helps you in your journey of finding a great dog trainer. We don't care who you train with as long as the end result is happy dogs and happy customers.

#10 - KEEP IT SIMPLE STUPID

When I was in the military, they loved using acronyms, and one of their favorites was KISS: Keep It Simple, Stupid. It's widely used, and it applies to dog training in every aspect. You need to keep every aspect of training simple, for both the dog and the owners. If it's too complicated for the dog, it'll take longer for them to understand. Likewise, if you make it complicated, the owner will struggle to get the dog to listen.

We offer our first lesson for just 50 cents, so owners can try it before committing. We get to tell them more about us. It's also

Want to open your own Make Your Dog Epic dog training business? Learn how to have your own! Open one of the most affordable and turn-key dog training businesses on the planet at MakeYourDogEpic.com.

a chance for us to learn about their dog and their goals because every dog is different, and everyone's goals are different.

To keep this short, a trainer had come out before for about five private lessons where they worked with the dog and client simultaneously. However, the mom recently called us because the behaviors were still happening. The dog was a 170-pound Great Dane, pulling so hard it would literally drag her down and then down the street. The only person in the house who could still take the dog on a walk was dad. I asked about the previous training, wanting to know what went wrong and what went well.

> "...CLIENTS DON'T WANT TO BECOME EXPERT DOG TRAINERS. THEY DON'T WANT TO INVEST THE MANY HOURS IT TOOK FOR YOU TO LEARN YOUR METHODS. THEY'RE PAYING YOU TO TRAIN THEIR DOG..."

The trainer had them using a prong collar, treats, and an e-collar all at the same time, which I understand is common for some trainers. The issue is that you shouldn't have to be a skilled handler to have a dog that listens. If someone is paying you to train them and their dog, the client shouldn't have to possess expert handling skills. Your training method should be so simple that even a typical six-year-old could get the dog to listen.

As a trainer, you have to understand that clients don't want to become expert dog trainers. They don't want to invest the many hours it took for you to learn your methods. They're paying you to train their dog and get it to listen to them. If you make it too complicated, nobody will be able to replicate your system, and you're doing them and their family a disservice. With every dog you train, you should imagine they'll need to listen to a 90-year-old grandma who can't raise her voice or be physical with the dog.

PAWS, for a Notable Quotable

"Practice does not make perfect. Only perfect practice makes perfect."

- VINCE LOMBARDI

(A man recognized as one of the greatest coaches in American football history.)

Want to open your own Make Your Dog Epic dog training business?
Learn how to have your own! Open one of the most affordable and turn-key dog training businesses on the planet at MakeYourDogEpic.com.

CHAPTER 8
Anxiety and Aggression

JOKE TIME
Q: What did the dog say to the sandpaper?
A: Ruff!

Before reading this, read the first chapter "Dogs See In Pictures".

This could be a whole book in itself. Instead of getting into the behaviorist side of things, trying to understand why the dog is doing something, I'm going to explain to you how we use training to fix and manage these behaviors. We are going to assume you have trained with us and now your dog understands and listens to commands. Now the next step, is behavior modification using those commands.

> **NOTE: IF THE DOG DOESN'T UNDERSTAND THE COMMANDS AND IS DOING THEM FOR THE FIRST TIME THEN THE BELOW WILL NOT WORK.**

The commands are going to be a tool that stops the bad behavior instantly, but the goal is to reshape the dog's picture of the situation. We are going to pick back up on the situation of the first chapter of going on a walk and your dog barks, growls or lunges at other dogs. When this is happening it is not necessary to understand what your dog is thinking. What I mean by this is the solution is still the same, it doesn't matter the underlying cause. If your dog is thinking "I need to protect mom" or "I want to play" or "I want to fight that dog" the solution is the same. We need to use the command "OFF" and or "COME". "OFF" means move away physically and mentally, but not that you are in trouble. This is key! We don't want your dog thinking you're mad or this other dog is bad, just "I need to move away".

Your dog starts barking and we say "OFF". The dog stops barking and turns away. You can be as strict or lenient as you want with this. One of our trainers can help you through it as well. Some dogs are so triggered or have been through so much trauma that they lose all privileges when it comes to other dogs. Sometimes even looking at the dog we tell them "OFF" so they aren't allowed to look. You will know your dog well. The moment you see your dog start working itself up you should say "OFF".

The result of doing this over and over is the dog's picture starts to get reshaped and the trigger disappears. The old picture was, "I see a dog I start barking and growling and I think I'm doing a good job because mom is saying things I don't understand". The new picture is "I see a dog. Mom is going to tell me to move away if I start barking, might as well not do it". Or the perfect reshaping of the picture is "I see a dog and now I'm no longer anxious or aggressive at all so I can play with them".

Want to open your own Make Your Dog Epic dog training business? Learn how to have your own! Open one of the most affordable and turn-key dog training businesses on the planet at MakeYourDogEpic.com.

The reason we offer our first lesson for 50 cents is so we can see your dog and hear your story and give you realistic expectations of where we can help you and your dog. We have had situations where people have almost given up hope and surrendered dogs, and we are able to come to that first lesson and completely change their life. This absolutely thrills us! Our whole goal is to give more freedom through dog training.

PAWS, for a Pro Tip

When dealing with people who break agreements and go against their word in order to maximize their profits, **RUN**!

PAWS, for a Notable Quotable

"Drifting, without aim or purpose, is the first cause of failure."

- NAPOLEON HILL
(Best-selling author of Think & Grow Rich.)

Want to open your own Make Your Dog Epic dog training business?
Learn how to have your own! Open one of the most affordable and turn-key dog training businesses on the planet at MakeYourDogEpic.com.

CHAPTER 9
Dog Quiz

JOKE TIME

Q: What do a dog and a cellphone have in common?
A: Both have collar ID!

This is a fun quiz you can do by yourself or challenge your family with! It will get harder as it goes on. Select the correct breed.

- A • Labrador retriever
- B • Chow Chow
- C • German Shepherd
- D • Seberian Husky

Golden Retriever • A
Bulldog • B
Border Collie • C
Australian Cattle dog • D

- A • Labrador retriever
- B • Chow Chow
- C • German Shepherd
- D • Seberian Husky

Want to open your own Make Your Dog Epic dog training business? Learn how to have your own! Open one of the most affordable and turn-key dog training businesses on the planet at MakeYourDogEpic.com.

Chow Chow · A
German Shepherd · B
Beagle · C
Akita · D

A · Belgian Malinois
B · French Bulldog
C · Australian Shepherd
D · Tibetan Mastiff

Australian Shepherd · A
Bedlington Terrier · B
Border Collie · C
Belgian Malinois · D

A · German Shepherd
B · Bull Terrier
C · Bedlington Terrier
D · Belgian Malinois

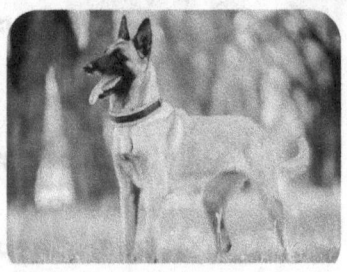

Want to open your own Make Your Dog Epic dog training business?
Learn how to have your own! Open one of the most affordable and turn-key dog training businesses on the planet at MakeYourDogEpic.com.

Chow Chow · A
Tibetan Mastiff · B
Akita · C
Irish wolfhound · D

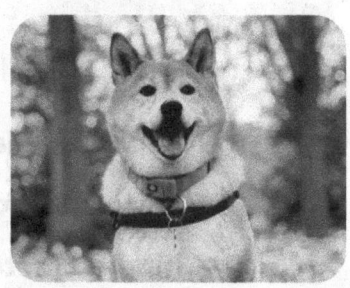

A · Akita
B · Irish wolfhound
C · Chow Chow
D · Tibetan Mastiff

Basset Hound · A
Neapolitan Mastiff · B
Shar Pei · C
Chinese crested · D

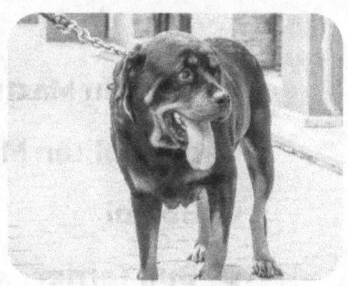

A · Chinese crested
B · Tibetan Mastiff
C · Neapolitan Mastiff
D · Rottweiler

Want to open your own Make Your Dog Epic dog training business?
Learn how to have your own! Open one of the most affordable and turn-key dog training businesses on the planet at MakeYourDogEpic.com.

12

Irish wolfhound · A
Brussels Griffon · B
Neapolitan Mastiff · C
Komondor · D

13

A · Shar Pei
B · Neapolitan Mastiff
C · Brussels Griffon
D · Chinese crested

14

German Shepherd · A
Seberian Husky · B
Shar Pei · C
Labrador Retriever · D

15

A · Tibetan Mastiff
B · Neapolitan Mastiff
C · Borzoi
D · Bull Terrier

Want to open your own Make Your Dog Epic dog training business?
Learn how to have your own! Open one of the most affordable and turn-key dog training businesses on the planet at MakeYourDogEpic.com.

16

Bedlington Terrier • A
Border Collie • B
Pig • C
Belgian Malinois • D

17

A • Prairie dog
B • Field Dog
C • Mountain Dog
D • Water Dog

18

Portuguese Mountain Dog • A
Portuguese Field Dog • B
Portuguese Prairie Dog • C
Portuguese Water Dog • D

PAWS,
for a Fun Fact

Dogs dream when
they sleep.
- *MentalFloss.com*

Want to open your own Make Your Dog Epic dog training business?
Learn how to have your own! Open one of the most affordable and turn-key dog training businesses on the planet at MakeYourDogEpic.com.

Correct Answers

1. D	7. D	13. D
2. A	8. A	14. C
3. C	9. A	15. B
4. C	10. A	16. C
5. B	11. B	17. A
6. A	12. A	18. D

PAWS, for a Notable Quotable

"Before success comes in any man's life, he is sure to meet with much temporary defeat, and, perhaps, some failure. When defeat overtakes a man, the easiest and most logical thing to do is to quit. That is exactly what the majority of men do. More than five hundred of the most successful men this country has ever known told the author their greatest success came just one step beyond the point at which defeat had overtaken them."

- NAPOLEON HILL

(Bestselling self-help author and the former apprentice of the world's wealthiest man, Andrew Carnegie.)

Want to open your own Make Your Dog Epic dog training business?
Learn how to have your own! Open one of the most affordable and turn-key dog training businesses on the planet at MakeYourDogEpic.com.

www.ingramcontent.com/pod-product-compliance
Lightning Source LLC
Chambersburg PA
CBHW010329030426
42337CB00025B/4875